PATHWAYS TO RECOVERY

Sources and Spiritual Tools

for a Jewish 12 Step Program

Second Edition

RABBI YAACOV J. KRAVITZ, ED.D.

The Center for Spiritual Intelligence Inc

Published by
The Center for Spiritual Intelligence Inc.
POB 30197, Elkins Park, PA 19027-0597
www.spiritualintelligence.com

Copyright © 2009. Rabbi Yaacov Jeffrey Kravitz, Ed.D, Center for Spiritual
Intelligence Inc.
First Edition 1997

Cataloging-in-Publication Data
Kravitz, Yaacov Jeffrey

Pathways To Recovery: Sources and Spiritual Tools for a Jewish 12 Step Program

ISBN 978-0-9815796-3-4   [Paper edition]

A Spiritual Intelligence®SM Publication

Author and Publisher's Note

The recommendations made in this book are generic and educational. They are not
meant to replace formal medical, psychological or psychiatric treatment. Individuals
with medical or psychological problems should consult with their physicians or
therapists about the appropriateness of the following program and discuss
appropriate modifications relevant to their unique circumstances and conditions.

Acknowledgements

This book would not have been written without the help of all the participants in SHOFAR. Their stories, struggles, questions and spiritual searches have provided the stimulus for bringing together the content of this book. Special thanks to Paula (OBM), Dave (OBM), Mary, Hope and Barry for your encouragement and support.

I also want to thank my wife Terry and sons Avi and Moshe whose love, support and sacrifice of family time also helped make this book a reality.

Contents

Appendices   77

Preface
A Journey into the 12 Steps

Recovering from addiction and developing a life filled with God and spirituality is not an easy task. However, the lonely path of recovery can be lightened and enlivened by a fellowship of like minded seekers. It was with these considerations in mind that I agreed to help start a support group for Jews in 12 Step programs in the Fall of 1992. I received a call from Shelly Johnson who was working at the Klein Branch of the Jewish Community Centers of Greater Philadelphia. Shelly informed me that a support group for Jews in 12 step programs called SHOFAR was operating at the Kaiserman Branch of the JCC under the direction of Janice Wilson. Shelly wanted to create a similar group in Northeast Philadelphia. She had heard that I was a rabbi and a psychologist who knew something about addictions and codependency. She asked me to be on the advisory board for the group. We met twice with three others and decided to have the first meeting in December of 1992. My intention was to help the group get started, provide some resources, and then slowly fade away into the background. As fate would have it, the participation of others faded and my role grew.

Working together with the group members a format was developed for our meetings. The first third of the meeting would be devoted to individual sharing of personal concerns related to recovery. The second segment would begin with the reading of the daily meditation from Rabbi Abraham Twersky's *Living Each Day,* followed by an opportunity for members to share their reactions to the meditation and to ask questions.

The final segment of the group was devoted to working the 12 steps from a Jewish perspective. Attempts to use several of the books available on the subject proved inadequate to the task. I began to bring in Jewish sources and to teach about Jewish spiritual practices related to each step. At each meeting more questions were asked about Jewish practice and belief. My responses to those questions were written down. Each time the group worked through the steps more questions were raised and what had been previously written was revised. It was through this process that *Pathways to Recovery* was born. The participation and insights of the group members added immensely to the richness of this book.

Along this pathway to recovery interesting things started to happen to group members. Some people were able to connect with their Higher Power for the first time. Some began to get in touch with their

Jewish heritage for the first time. After two years in SHOFAR and thirteen years in recovery one member even decided to have a recovery *bar mitzvah*.

My personal experience in the group was also interesting. While I had not intended to continue to attend weekly meetings, I became devoted to the group. I kept coming back because I loved being with a group of Jews who wanted to talk about and develop their own spirituality. I had tried to do this at other times in my career in the pulpit rabbinate, on campus and in Jewish education but nowhere else had I found such phenomenal responsiveness to and yearning for teaching about God and Judaism. So I came and I worked the steps myself. I had known about the steps and had done work on some of them, but I had never worked through all the steps systematically.

This work appealed to my soul. Here was an opportunity teach and to attend to my own spiritual growth and recovery. If I was going to teach about the Jewish dimension or approach to recovery I had to be willing to "walk the walk and not just talk the talk." My rabbinic education had prepared me for the intellectual and teaching aspects of the program, and I had been exposed to spiritual and personal growth opportunities through my pastoral psychology work and my learning with Rabbi Zalman Schachter-Sholomi. SHOFAR was an ideal setting for testing what I had learned and continuing my personal integration of the insights of Judaism and psychology.

Group members had decided to call the group SHOFAR, an acronym standing for Self-Help Organization for Addiction and Recovery. Additionally, *shofar* also refers to the ram's horn which is blown on the Hebrew New Year to arouse individuals to do a deep soul-searching and turning towards God. That is ultimately what recovery from addiction is about. The word "addiction" literally means to give oneself over to something. Recovery is about making a commitment to one's Higher Power and giving up your addiction. When the *shofar* is blown we are called to let its piercing sound penetrate our souls, to turn from our misdeeds and return to our true selves. Each SHOFAR meeting provided those attending with the opportunity and tools for making the journey back to their true self and to their Higher Power.

How to Use This Book

This book is intended as a resource for both groups and individuals. For each step I have provided a general introduction to the step from a Jewish perspective, Jewish sources related to the step and a variety of ways to approach the process of doing the step. It is highly recommended that you keep a journal while reading *Pathways to Recovery*. Use your journal to write down your reactions, thoughts, and questions as you work each step. You can then bring your journal to your sponsor, mentor, or rabbi for further discussion.

When you begin each step, start by reading the general introduction. Use your journal to note your reactions or simply write them in the margins of the book. Go through the sources, again noting any questions or problems that arise. It is vital that you have a rabbi or teacher who can go over this material with you when questions arise. Do not hesitate to consult with someone else. I have often been amazed to see how easily certain sources can be misinterpreted or misunderstood by well meaning and intelligent people who simply lack some important background information. While I have tried to provide much of that information, it is impossible to anticipate every question.

In the SHOFAR group the general introduction would be used to begin our work on each step. Usually discussion and questions followed. During this section of the meeting the rule about cross talk did not apply in order to allow for a free exchange of ideas. At the next meeting the group would review a few of the sources and begin to work on one of the suggested approaches to doing the step. That work might involve doing one of the guided meditations or simply spending some time writing about personal responses to the step.

Notes on Doing Imagery Exercises

In the Process section of many of the steps, I have utilized guided meditations. A word of instruction is necessary. Read through each meditation several times, then begin by closing your eyes and going through it step by step. Some people find it desirable to read the meditation into a tape recorder or have someone with a pleasant voice tape it for them. Whenever you see a series of periods ... that indicates you should pause for 5 or 10 seconds to give your mind a chance to play with the images. For those who do not see images visually, simply guide your thoughts along the direction indicated.

A Note on Language

Throughout this book I endeavored to achieve a balance in use of gendered language. Rather than alternate him and her I have often chosen to use him/her in spite of its awkwardness. It should be noted that Him/Her has been applied to certain cases where it was necessary to use a pronoun for God in order to indicate that God has no gender. However, Him/Her as applied to God might imply a sense of duality, so I have also alternated Him and Her.

In working with some Hebrew phrases and blessings I have chosen not to translate the scared four letter name of God from the Hebrew, but to use the traditional "*HaShem.*" *HaShem* simply means "The Name." It is used in Hebrew when referring to God outside of the context of actual prayer in order to avoid speaking God's name lightly or in vain. The four letter name of God, pronounced *A-do-nai* in prayer, is masculine and the use of *HaShem* provides a gender neutral alternative. During your actual prayer it is recommended that you utilize the traditional pronunciation. If a feminine alternative is desired, Rabbi Mordecai Kaplan has suggested the use of *Yah*, a feminine form of God's name found frequently in the Bible. In translating, I have chosen to use plain, descriptive language, consistent with the context of recovery.

Introduction
A Jewish 12 step model

The story of the exodus of the children of Israel from Egypt is a model for a Jewish view of addiction and recovery. Egypt (*mitzrayim* in Hebrew) literally means 'the double narrow place.' It is the place where the Hebrews were given over into slavery. Addiction comes from a Latin root meaning 'to give oneself over'. Addiction is slavery. On a very personal level then, the story of the Exodus from Egypt is the personal story of each Jew coming out of his or her narrow place, out of their addiction. The telling of the Exodus story is repeated countless times each day by each recovering person speaking in his or her 12 step meeting. It is with this background in mind that we begin our examination of the recovery process from a Jewish perspective, looking closely at the Exodus story to see what it can teach us about addiction and recovery.

There comes a time in both slavery and addiction when one can no longer bear the situation. This is the time when, in the words of step 1, we realize that we are powerless over our addiction and that life is unmanageable. An allusion to this preliminary step to recovery and redemption is found in the exodus story where we are told that, "it came to pass that the King of Egypt died and the Children of Israel groaned because of their burden and they cried out; their cry came up to God from their slavery." (Exodus 2:23)

The Children of Israel were simply stuck in their slavery. All they could do was to cry, rather than taking any effective action. Sometimes we simply cry and complain about the unmanageability of our lives and our addiction. There are many people who are stuck in step 1 just as the Children of Israel were stuck in their slavery. It is not until we come to believe that a Higher Power can help us and we begin to act upon that belief that things start to happen. Step 2 is the glimmer of hope that slavery and unmanageability can be transformed into freedom and sanity.

True redemption and sanity are possible only when people give themselves over to God, coming to the realization that personal recovery is possible only in reaching beyond the self. This act of surrender is the basis for Step 3, making a decision to turn our will and our lives over to the care of God as we understand Him/Her. On the first Passover our ancestors had to totally renounce their dependence on slavery and turn their lives over to God in order to be ready to be taken out of Egypt. The verse in the Torah which

5

describes that turning to God states, "Moses called to all the elders of Israel, saying to them: `Draw out and take a lamb for each of your families, and slaughter the Passover (lamb).'" (Exodus 12:21) The connection between this strange act and turning one's life over to God is explained in the *Midrash* (Rabbinic legend) which states:

> When the Holy One, blessed be He, told Moses to slay the Passover lamb, Moses answered: `Lord of the Universe! How can I possibly do that?  Do You not know that the lamb is the Egyptian god?' … God replied: `Israel will not depart from here before they slaughter the Egyptian gods before their very eyes, that I may teach them that their gods are really nothing at all.' This is what He actually did; for on that night He slew the Egyptian firstborn and on that night the Israelites slaughtered their paschal lamb and ate it.

[*Midrash Rabbah, Parshat* Bo XVI, 3]

Redemption was merited by Israel after they put aside other gods and turned to *HaShem*.

In Judaism turning to God is a great act of faith. This turning to God and away from addiction is part the process of *teshuvah* or repentance, which in its literal biblical form simply means "turning." The 12 steps are about a process which is similar in many ways to *teshuvah*. The purpose of this book is to explore this process and provide spiritual tools for healing from addiction.

Teshuvah and the 12 step program are both spiritual in nature, although the way each one defines spirituality is different. Twelve step spirituality focuses on each individual's relationship to his or her Higher Power. Everyone has their own unique path to that spirituality. My definition of spirituality in Judaism is based on a saying of the sages that "The world is based on three things: *Torah, Avodah, and Gemilut hasadim*."[1] *Torah* refers to the Hebrew Bible and the wisdom of our sages. *Torah* is about having a moral and ethical path. It is about having values which are shared with other Jews. *Avodah* refers to service to God, having a relationship with God and having meaning and purpose in life. *Gemilut hasadim* are deeds of loving kindness, the way we relate to the members of our community and all human kind. The practice of *Gemilut hasadim* points to the fact that recovery is not done in isolation, but must occur in the context of a loving community.

Transposing this saying into a more modern idiom we would say that spirituality is about moving powerfully towards your life goals
with a **HEART** that is open and flexible,

with **E**nthusiasm,
with **A**wareness of your present experience and of the presence of the
divine in all,
with **R**espect for and service to others and the world, and
guided by the **T**raditions of your highest values.

HEART is used heart as an acronym with each letter referring to
specific qualities or abilities that together comprise what I have called
"spiritual intelligence."[2]

The process of spiritual healing is a process of moving from
brokenness to wholeness (*shalom or shleimut*). When we live in the world
of addiction God's face is hidden from us. In a very fundamental way the
hidden face of *HaShem* represents the natural order of things. It is the base
line of living as creatures in a material world. When we seek *HaShem's* face
we bring His Mercy into the world and experience Healing and Redemption.
In addiction we experience the full force of Natural Law. Our lives are
unmanageable and lack true sparks of joy and love. It is only in turning to
God that we experience the attribute of God's Mercy and Love. It is through
the processes of *teshuvah* and recovery that we actually play a part in
bringing a Divine Presence into the world. The details of how you will
accomplish this feat are to be found in the steps and in the emotional and
spiritual work you are about to begin.

STEP 1

We admitted we were powerless over our addiction - that our lives had become unmanageable

It is the unmanageability of our lives and the associated disappoint-ments, lies and feelings of emptiness that give us the first clue that we have a problem. This spiritual headache is a symptom which directs our attention to the problem - our addiction. We realize that we have made an addiction the center of our lives, that it controls us and makes our lives bitter. Addictions seem to have a momentum of their own. The Sages referred to this when they said, "*Mitzvah goreret mitzvah, aveirah goreret aveirah*" - One *mitzvah* (a sacred deed) follows another, one evil (addictive) behavior follows another." [3] We easily get into bad habits and addictions and it is only with much hard work that we are able to forge a new path.

The basic imperative of Step 1 is that you must look reality in the eye. All of the excuses, lies and deceptions may have worked in the short term, but they have provided only fleeting relief and have often created more problems than they solved. All of the previous strategies that you have tried have not led to a lasting solution to the problem of addiction. Step 1 says with utter simplicity that you acknowledge that are at the end of your rope and that life is unmanageable.

Many individuals who suffer from addiction are under the illusion that they have a large measure of control over the addiction, over their efforts to stop the addiction and over their own lives and the lives of those closest to them. Step 1 reflects the awareness that this sense of control and our attempts to control are fleeting and partial at best. The illusion of control is actually part of the problem rather than part of the solution. It is only when we admit our powerlessness and see clearly that our attempts to control addiction and life have not worked, that we are ready to explore the path called recovery. Paradoxically, we will have to learn that recovery is not about control. We will learn that recovery is about our willingness to accept what we cannot change, and our commitment to move powerfully towards our goals in life guided by our highest values and our Higher Power.

Step 1, the awareness of a problem, takes place in solitude, within the confines of one's broken heart and spirit. The discomfort which results from this awareness will become articulated and expanded as we speak with friends and enter the 12-step program.

SOURCES:

Step 1 begins with a realization that one is out of balance. It is finally breaking through our denial and minimization of our problems. We can come to this realization in many ways.

1. Rabbenu Yona teaches that there are six means by which a person may awaken himself to turn aside from his evil ways:
    a] when many troubles come upon a man he should commune with his heart, acknowledging that they are the fruits of his ways and actions and that his sins have brought them upon him; and he should return to God who will be compassionate to him.
    b] the realization in old age of one's approaching end
    c] acceptance of words of reproof
    d] learning Torah
    e] the ten Days of Repentance and Yom Kippur
    f] constant preoccupation with repentance in anticipation of death.[4]

PROCESS*: Doing Step 1   (Write individually and share in group)*

1. Examine the ways in which you are powerless, out of balance, and your life is unmanageable. Most people find it helpful to keep a 12 step journal for recording their step work. Write out your answers to the following questions:

    A] What are your narrow places, your addictions?

    _____
    _____
    _____
    _____
    _____
    _____
    _____
    _____

    B] How are you powerless over your addiction(s)? List all the things that you have tried to stop your addiction that have not worked.

    _____
    _____
    _____
    _____
    _____
    _____
    _____
    _____

    C] How do your addictive behaviors make your life unmanageable? How have your addictions affected your work and relationships?

    _____
    _____
    _____
    _____
    _____
    _____
    _____
    _____

2. Viewing the Old and the New You.

    Try the following imagery exercise. (For those who do not see images visually, simply guide your thoughts along the direction indicated)

    Sit down and relax... Get comfortable... Close your eyes... Take three slow breaths, taking longer to exhale than to inhale...

    See yourself watching a TV tuned to your own channel.... See yourself in your addiction, acting it out. See in some detail what your life is like.... See how you are powerless and how your life is unmanageable....how your life is not in balance...

    See which of your needs and wants are being satisfied...

    See what is out of order...

    Now, change the channel. See yourself out of your addiction and in recovery...

    Notice what has changed...

    Notice how you go about meeting your needs in an appropriate way or how you get help if you are in trouble...

    Notice how it might feel to be in recovery...

    Take a moment to enjoy this and to imagine how you might have gotten there...

    Take three more breaths. ...

    Open your eyes.

    If this exercise is done in a group setting, take time to share with a partner, or with the whole group, some of your reactions. You can share either details of the experience or what you learned from the experience as a whole. Remember not to comment on anyone else's experience. You acknowledge the experience simply by listening.

3. Life Values Review

    Imagine that you are now approaching the day of your death. Look over your life as you have lived it until now - in your addiction. What regrets do you have? Write down how you feel about what you have done and accomplished in your life. What are the values that you would now like to see embodied in your life?

    _____

    _____

    _____

STEP 2

Came to believe that a Power greater than ourselves could restore us to sanity.

Sanity is the sense that our lives are manageable and have direction. Our lives become unmanageable because we lack a true center. In addiction one focuses on self gratification. In codependency one focuses on gratifying others. In recovery we turn our sights to serving our Higher Power. Only then are we able to balance meeting our own needs in an appropriate way with joyfully extending ourselves for others. That balance is what some people call sanity.

People who have become depressed about their addiction or try to commit suicide have given up hope and feel helpless. They feel they have no reason to live. Having a goal in life, a value for which we will sacrifice all, or a purpose we strive to fulfill, is one of the keys to getting through any difficulty. Holocaust survivor and psychiatrist Viktor Frankl based his entire method of psychotherapy on this basic principle. A sane person has a center and a direction. Both are lost in addiction.

We pray for God's help and simultaneously open ourselves to that help. Only through belief in a Higher Power and commitment to serving a purpose in life can we be helped to transcend our addiction. In the process of opening ourselves to help we are helped by using the tools of our group, our community and our study of our tradition as paths to our Higher Power. We know that whatever we have tried to do before to fight our addiction has not worked. Step 2 signals that it is time to try something totally new.

Step 2 is traditionally one of the hardest steps for liberal Jews. Belief in a Higher Power has become difficult for Jews living in the modern world. Two factors have conspired against our belief in God: materialism, and our aversion to non-Jewish forms of spirituality. The assumption of early twentieth century science that we would eventually explain everything through scientific study desensitized us to the spiritual dimension of life. Rodger Kamenetz, author of *The Jew in the Lotus*, speaks elegantly about how he rejected spirituality because it was associated with faith healers and charismatic preachers. Anything so *goyish* had to be *treif.*

Rabbi Mordecai Kaplan has made a useful distinction between belief in God and our concept of God. Our belief in God or a Higher Power is that gut feeling that there is a Power greater than ourselves. It is more of a feeling than a thought, inspired by an evening gazing at the stars, being present at the birth of a child, or being inexplicably rescued from the certain disaster of our addiction.

Our *concept* of God is our attempt to articulate in some coherent fashion just what that Higher Power is. God concepts are influenced by personal history, family, religion and culture. Jewish God concepts have been influenced by the historical encounter of the Jewish people with God. While we steadfastly maintain a belief that there is one God, Jews have talked about and experienced that God in a variety of ways through history.

The problem we often encounter in Step 2 is that while we have a basic belief in God, we have encountered numerous difficulties trying to articulate a concept of God that makes sense. For the purpose of doing step 2 it is sufficient to believe that there is a Power Greater than ourselves which can return us to sanity. There is no need at this point to have a fully articulated concept of God. Sometimes it is not our Higher Power that restores us to sanity, but our belief itself that opens us up to healing. This idea is often expressed by the saying heard at 12 step meetings, "fake it until you make it."

An additional problem distancing modern Jews from the language of spirituality is that English is a Christian language. Terms that we commonly use such as holy, sacred, grace, and surrender often seem to have a Christian connotation. The Lord's Prayer said at many 12 step meetings sounds very Christian even though it has roots in Jewish tradition. Because these words sound so Christian, they often become a source of discomfort when Jews try to talk about spirituality. We can reclaim spirituality by learning a few basic Hebrew terms which will open the doors of spiritual recovery.

The traditional God images of the monotheistic religions may bring to mind the idea of God as the Ultimate Controller. People who have experienced chaotic, addictive families find the image of a benevolent Ultimate Controller totally unfamiliar. Feeling alone and abandoned in a chaotic environment it is only natural to reach for whatever control may be available. Attempts to control the uncontrollable through avoidance, or trying to be in control through addiction are efforts doomed to failure. While these attempts may seem to work in the short term we ultimately discover that they only lead us into insanity. The belief that a Higher Power can restore sanity is really an extension of the Step 1 belief that we are powerless and not really in control. Discovering what it is like to live without trying to be in control is what the Twelve Steps are all about.

As you study the texts presented here and elsewhere, as you see how others relate to their Higher Power, and as you see how your Higher Power works in your own life, you will be able to develop a growing sense of spirituality and your own concept of God. In much the same way that as we mature we have to work to develop the skills to use our emotions constructively, spirituality must be nurtured through positive modeling, learning and experience.

SOURCES:

1. My God, My God, why have you forsaken me?
   So far from saving me, from the words of my groaning?
   0 my God, I cry by day, but you do not answer;
   and by night, but find no rest.
   Yet you are holy, enthroned on the praises of Israel.
   In You our ancestors trusted; they trusted, and You delivered them.
   To You they cried, and were saved;
   in You they trusted, and were not ashamed. (Psalm 22)

   > The message from Psalm 22 echoes what was referred to in
   > our earlier discussion. When we are feeling at our lowest and
   > most unmanageable, we may feel far from God. At this time it
   > is good to remember that others have walked this path before
   > us. Our ancestors and those who entered the 12 step program
   > before us found a path to recovery. If we follow in their
   > footsteps we too can attain recovery even if we feel forsaken
   > at the present time.

2. All the world is a narrow bridge, and the main thing is not to be afraid.
   (Rebbe Nachman of Bratzlov)
3. A person's temptation becomes more intense each day, and were it not
   that God helps him, it would be impossible to resist. (Talmud: Sukkah
   52b)[5]
4. Lord of Hosts, happy is the person who trusts in you. (Psalm 84:13)
5. Serve *HaShem* in joy, come before Him in gladness. (Psalm 100)
6. The foundation of all foundations and basis of all science is to know that
   there is a First Cause who has brings forth everything into being.
   (Maimonides, *Mishneh Torah*: *Fundamentals of the Torah*, Chapter 1,
   Halakhah 1)
7. I lift my eyes to the mountains. What is the source of my help?
   My help comes from *HaShem*, Maker of heaven and earth.
   HaShem will not let your foot give way; your Guardian will not slumber.
   See, the Guardian of Israel neither slumbers nor sleeps!
   HaShem is your Guardian, *HaShem* is your protection at your right hand.
   The sun will not strike you by day, nor the moon by night.
   HaShem will guard you from all evil; *HaShem* will guard your soul,
   your going out and coming, from now until forever.
   (Psalm 121)

8. Without my trust in *HaShem* I would never perceive His goodness in this world. Hope in *HaShem*. Strengthen and encourage yourself and continue to hope in *HaShem*.   (Psalm 27: 13-14)

PROCESS: Doing Step 2

1. Thinking about you Higher Power.
   Write about this step in your journal and talk about it in your regular 12 Step meeting. Here are some questions to get you started.

   A] Do you believe there is a Higher Power? What experiences form the basis of your belief?

   _____

   _____

   _____

   _____

   _____

   _____

   _____

   _____

   B] What values or ideals do you hold that make life worth living or that give purpose to your life?

   _____

   _____

   _____

   _____

   _____

   _____

   _____

   C] Describe some positive actions you can take that will move you in the direction of living consistently with your belief in a Higher Power and/or your values/ideals.

   _____

   _____

   _____

   _____

   _____

D] If you are having difficulty with this step, what keeps you from making a commitment to your Higher Power or your values?

_____

_____

_____

_____

_____

2. Learning about how to think about your Higher Power.
   Talk to a rabbi about the different ways in which God has been conceptualized in Judaism.

3. Spend some time meditating on one of the verses or psalms cited in the Sources.

4. This step is often hard to see and imagine as an actual change in belief. Try the following imagery exercise. (For those who do not see images visually, simply guide your thoughts along the direction indicated.)

   Sit down and relax... Get comfortable... Close your eyes...
   Take three slow breaths, taking longer to exhale than to inhale...
   See yourself in a comfortable safe place, watching a TV tuned to your own channel. See yourself in your addiction, acting it out.... See in some detail what your life is like there and how your addiction affects what you do, what you say, and how you relate to others....
   Now, change the channel to a time in the future, a future life channel. See yourself there in recovery with a belief in a Higher Power.... See what you do, how you relate to others and to your Higher Power. Feel how this affects you and how it is different from being in addiction....
   Let yourself know that anytime you need to do step 2, you can pick up the remote and turn to this channel.
   Take three more breaths....
   Open your eyes, and come back to the room.

   Write your reactions to this exercise below.
   If this exercise is done in a group setting take time to share with a partner, or with the whole group, some of your reactions.

_____

_____

_____

_____

Step 3:
Made a decision to turn our will and our lives over to the care of God as we understand Him/Her

Step 3 represents a choice to attach oneself to something greater than self with the realization that you will no longer turn your will and life over to your addiction. This act of turning to God is known as *Teshuvah* - literally "turning." The decision made is not something done once and then forgotten. It is a decision which one renews continually. The nature and quality of this decision will change as one's understanding of God grows and changes. At the beginning you may experience only a change of spirit. As your relationship to God and the Jewish people changes you may make further changes in the people, places, and things with whom and with which you associate. For others this sequence may be reversed. A change in spirit may follow a change in behavior.

To strengthen your decision to turn your will over to the care of God you may decide to act in ways which reflect your new center of life. The specific actions that you take each and every day reflect the values that you consciously or unconsciously are committed to. Values refer to the thoughts or beliefs that we hold to be most important in life. The values we have reflect individual experience, and the traditions and beliefs of our family, culture, ethnic group and religion. Our most important values involve not only what we profess verbally to ourselves or others, but what we act on repeatedly. In religions and cultures values may come to be expressed as rules, guidelines, or laws.

In Judaism the actions connecting us to our values and our Higher Power are called *mitzvoth* (commandments or connectors); e.g., lighting Sabbath candles, supporting our community, observing the Sabbath, treating others with love and respect. Each activity of the day provides an opportunity for doing a *mitzvah* and turning one's will over to God. The supreme expression of turning one's life to God is represented by *mesirat nefesh* (literally, 'turning over one's soul') or martyrdom. For now, we need only be concerned about turning in the right direction.

Organized religions have addressed the connection between values and action by praising and rewarding specific deeds which seem to reflect related values. For example, compassion may be demonstrated in numerous ways including giving charity, feeding the hungry, doing favors for others or volunteer work. Values are also frequently embodied in the rituals that surround important holidays and life cycle events.

When values are expressed through our speech and action we are making an important behavioral connection between our Higher Power and our own spiritual center. The performance of any action can be accompanied by the recitation of a blessing which acknowledges God's presence in the moment. The universal practice of blessing is an acknowledgment of God's presence in the moment that can serve to remind us of our decision to turn our will and all our life over to the care of God as we understand Him/Her. Each activity of the day provides an opportunity for acknowledging the miracle of life and for turning one's will over to God. The practice of mindfully blessing the present moment and acknowledging God presents us with a powerful counter-balance to the impulsive and mindless acting out of our addiction.

My favorite model for turning my life over to God is the Sabbath. All week long I am busy doing what I want to do, going places, writing, working, exercising, running errands, checking e-mail and more. On Shabbat that all comes to a halt. No matter how urgent the work or other responsibilities everything is put on hold for 25 hours. For one day each week I take time to reconnect with God by disconnecting with work. Shabbat is a time for re-souling, time to meditate, be with the family, enjoy nature, relax, and celebrate with friends. It is a day when I let go of control and simply enjoy the world as it has been created.

Another way to think about the decision to turn your will over to God is that it is the beginning of a decision to do what God wants you to do. As we will learn in Step 11 there are clear guidelines for determining God's will for us. Part of God's will for us is that we are responsible for making the hard moral choices which often confront us. Once your decision has been made what is different is that you can continue on your life's path strengthened by a faith and a direction which was previously foreign to you. The Psalmist hinted at this when he stated, "Were it not for my faith in the Lord, I would be unable to see God's goodness in the world."[6] Knowing what your Higher Power stands for and what your values are provides you with a moral compass helping you determine whether you are moving in the direction of addiction or recovery.

Turning one's life and will over to God is the hardest part of the first three steps. Often we resist steps 2 and 3. This resistance may reflect our difficulties with our intellectual understanding of God, with traditional images of God (e.g. male images), or with our personal images of God (problems of willfulness, control issues, or issues with authority).

Intellectually, many modern Jews question Step 3 in the context of life after the Holocaust. They ask, "How can I turn my life over to a God who abandoned my people in our darkest hour?" This question is echoed on a personal level for many who have suffered abuse, chronic illness or disability.

A complete response to the question of the justice of God is clearly beyond the scope of this work. There are numerous scholarly attempts to deal with this topic. Harold Kushner's *When Bad Things Happen to Good People* has been one response which many of my addicted and abused clients have found helpful.

The Jewish beliefs in the free will of each individual and the constancy of the laws of nature suggest that there are limits to the degree a personal God will intervene in the affairs of humankind. However, along with those ideas comes the belief that God is with those who suffer. This idea is reflected in a rabbinic homily which begins by asking why God revealed Himself to Moses in a small burning thorn bush, rather than in a majestic display of thunder and lightning as He did later for the Jewish people on Mt. Sinai. The rabbis respond by saying that God wished to teach us that even as the people of Israel suffered in slavery in Egypt, God was with them in their suffering, as symbolized by God's speaking to Moses from the midst of the thorns.

Some people have questioned their own belief in God because they were unable to find an understandable and sympathetic concept of God. Some strands of Jewish tradition have used anthropomorphic images to articulate a concept of God, while others maintain that God has no body and is not a person. The rabbis of the Talmud tell us that the Torah speaks in the language of humans so that we may have a way to relate to God who is really beyond our capacity to understand. Because of the substantial difficulties involved in conceptualizing God as a supra human and supra moral entity some scholars have entirely rejected the idea of supernatural God.[7] If God is all powerful yet evil exists in the world, then God forfeits His role as a moral force worthy of our imitation. In order to have a morally understandable and imitable God we must move from inquiries into His incomprehensible nature to a search for the qualities and actions that represent holiness. The traditional God as Supernatural Being is replaced by human responsibility for acting in a godlike fashion.

Those who reject such a radical reconstruction may still need to examine their images of God. The most frequent Jewish images are those of God as Creator of the Universe, Redeemer, and Revealer of the Torah. Other images of God abound, for example, warrior, punisher, avenger, healer, savior, awesome, mighty, helper, and protector. All of the images just mentioned are based on human experiences. Some of them may not be comprehensible to you, or be compatible with your way of thinking. That need not negate your belief in a Higher Power. Use your experience and

21

study Jewish texts to find what you do value and use that as a starting point for developing a meaningful concept of a Higher Power that provides you with a livable model of holiness.

Our earliest images of God do not come from any book and are not learned in school. They come from our earliest experiences in life with our parents who represent our first encounter with a Higher Power. Our parents are the first ones to teach us about love, trust, and protection. What we learn in the cradle in our formative years shapes the way we see life, the world and God. These images are often unconscious or preconscious. Thus, if our earliest experiences in life have given us a view of the world as a chaotic, vengeful place, we may have incorporated those images into our image of God. We will be quite hesitant about turning our lives over to the care of such a God. Some people are able to avoid this pitfall, but I have found it to be relatively common among those in recovery.

The lack of feminine images of God is problematic for many recovering Jewish women. It is sometimes helpful to know that there is also a feminine aspect of God. The traditional image of the *Schechinah*, the Indwelling Presence of God, is feminine. That feminine image is associated in later Kabbalistic thought with the concept of *Malchut* (Sovereignty), one of the ten *sefirot* or emanations of God.

Theological objections and questions of belief should be taken seriously, but one should be alert for their potential misuse as a defense against dealing with one's feelings. The distinction between theological and personal issues is sometimes difficult to make. If you just can't seem to get through Step 3 this might be a good time to seek the help of your therapist or rabbi. These issues may need to be resolved before you can take Step 3.

Because of the difficulty involved in Step 3 it may be useful to ask two simple questions: What has stopped you from doing step 3? How have you stopped yourself from doing the work of Step 3?

The most common barriers to doing step 3 are anger, fear, unwillingness to give up control, and lack of self forgiveness. One SHOFAR member's comments were quite moving, "If I do these steps I have to look at what I have done. I don't like my past and I don't want to face it." This individual felt that his past was so repugnant that he could never be forgiven by God and he could never be a better person. This attitude represents an underestimation of the power of *teshuvah*. When a person turns to God with all of their thoughts, feelings and deeds it is really as if they had become a new person. The power of *Teshuvah* is that when we do our part through turning, God is certain to do Her part by granting forgiveness and acceptance.

SOURCES:

1.   Cast your burden upon the Lord and He will sustain you; He will never let the righteous collapse. (Psalm 55:23)

   Rabbi Twersky[8] interprets this verse from Psalms to mean that we should turn over to God all of the burdens which confront us, all the things we cannot change. Our responsibility, on the other hand, is to achieve righteousness by changing the things we can change.

2.   Give over into the hand of the Holy One, blessed be He, everything that is yours, because it is all His. And by doing so you will not be pained by any loss that comes to you.

   (*Or haNer* #42, quoted in M. Buxbaum, *Jewish Spiritual Practices*, p. 675.)

3.   Rabban Gamaliel used to say:
   Make His (God's) will as if it was your will
   so that He will make your will His will.
   Annul your will before His will
   so that He will annul the will of others before your will.
   (Ethics of the Fathers 2:4)

   This pithy statement might be considered an ancient statement of step 3, however it needs additional explanation:
   Do His will as if it was your will - Do each of the *mitzvoth* (the expression of *HaShem*'s will) as though this is truly your will. Put as much time and effort into doing *mitzvoth* as you would into your own interests. Acting responsibly and consistently according to your highest values is an expression of doing God's will.

4.   Into God's hands I deliver my spirit
   when I sleep and wake
   with my spirit and my being
   God is with me and I will not fear.

   This beautiful phrase is taken from the song *Adon Olam* (Master of the World). It is found in the Jewish prayer book and often sung at either the beginning or end of every morning service. Some prayer books include it among the prayers which are said before going to sleep at night.

PROCESS: *Doing Step 3*

1. Talk in group or write in your journal about Step 3. Any of the following questions may be used to guide your discussion or writing.

   A] What are your images of and thoughts about a Higher Power?

   _____
   _____
   _____
   _____
   _____
   _____
   _____
   _____

   B] Do you need to change your concept of Higher Power to make it more accessible to you? If so, what changes will you make?

   _____
   _____
   _____
   _____
   _____
   _____
   _____
   _____

   C] Have you made a decision to turn your will and life over to the care of your Higher Power? If so, how has it affected you?

   _____
   _____
   _____
   _____
   _____
   _____
   _____
   _____

2. If you have difficulty with this step work on these tasks:
    a. Separate your belief in God (gut feeling or knowing that there is a Higher Power) from your concept of God (how you express it).
    b. Separate personal images and personal issues with authority figures from your image of God. If you have difficulty with this and are stuck on steps 1-3 talk to a rabbi, a Jewish pastoral counselor or a therapist who understands religious issues and the 12 steps.

3. We can make our daily language reflect our decision to turn our lives over to *HaShem*. Use the following phrases at every opportunity throughout the day. They can serve as arrows to direct our awareness back to the central role of our Higher Power.[9]
    a. *Im yirtzeh HaShem* - God willing
    b. *B' ezrat HaShem* - With the help of God
    c. *Baruch HaShem* - Blessed (or acknowledged) is God. (The traditional response to the greeting, "How are you?")
    d. *Halleluyah* - Praise *HaShem*

4. Try the following imagery exercise after doing all of the above.
    Put your feet flat on the floor.   Relax...   Get comfortable... Close your eyes... Take three slow breaths, taking longer to exhale than to inhale...
    See yourself in a wide open, beautiful prairie... Notice the grass...feel it brush against you.   See the   many varieties of flowers, red, yellow, purple. Smell the fresh scent of the prairie.... Walk through the prairie and feel the breeze against your skin. Is it warm or cool? As you continue to walk you might notice that there is a path just ahead which quickly separates into several forks. Choose one of the paths and follow it ... As you continue to walk the path begins to take you up a steep incline and the air begins to get misty. You have difficulty seeing, but you can continue to make out your way. As the mist gets thicker you begin to notice that it is really quite pleasant and comforting. You begin to notice a strong, yet gentle presence around you, guiding your steps and watching out for you...... As you continue walking you realize that this Presence might be one of the ways you experience your Higher Power... Let go... Let go as you turn yourself over to the care of your Higher Power. Experience what this is like for you, knowing that at any time you choose to end this experience you can simply open your eyes.
    Keeping your awareness of your Higher Power with you, begin now to return to the prairie... Let yourself know that whenever you need help

you can close your eyes, repeat this meditation and return to this meadow. For now, take three more breaths and let your eyes open. [10]

Write about your response to this exercise in your journal and/or share your response with your group. Was the experience pleasant or upsetting? Did you experience any resistance to letting go? What would it mean to let go in this way in your daily life?

_____

_____

_____

_____

_____

_____

_____

_____

5. The following prayer is adapted from the traditional *Amidah*, the standing meditation which is recited three times each day.[11] It is not part of the original prayer, but an optional addition to one of the *Amidah*'s nineteen blessings. The prayer is a personal petition suggesting that we seek to turn over to God the provision of all of our needs, especially our food. Recital of this prayer can help to cultivate an attitude of appreciation for our dependence on God as the Creator and Provider of all.

> It is You *HaShem*, our Higher Power, who nourishes, prospers and enlivens all, from microbe to galaxy. Please continue to sustain this process of life and growth; provide me with my portion of nourishment, preparing all for me and my family even before we are aware of the need … so that I can do Your will, be involved in your Torah, and fulfill Your commandments, setting up connections with You in order to live in constant awareness of Your Presence. Fulfill for me the Scripture which states: "You open Your hand, and satisfy the desires of all living things," (Psalm 145:16) as well as the Scripture "Cast your burden upon the Lord and He will sustain you." (Psalm 55:23)

Introduction to Steps 4 - 9

In steps 1, 2 and 3 we turned our lives in a new direction. Our work was primarily work of the heart and of will. Now comes the time to do the hard work of *teshuvah* making the rest of our lives consistent with our decision. Steps 4 through 9 are about doing *teshuvah* for our misdeeds. The Hebrew word for misdeed or sin is *Chet*. *Chet* literally means 'to miss the mark,' as when one shoots a bow and arrow. In our addiction we shot our arrows and then drew a target around them to justify our actions. Now we do the hard work of learning to aim for a target which exists outside of our own desires.

The first three steps focused on the awareness that the center of power for our lives must be our Higher Power rather than our addiction. In order to maintain this focus we must identify what our values are and how we can live a life consistent with those values. When we speak of values we are not talking about specific objectives like having specific career, a fancy house or even having a family with three children. Each of these examples of an objective represents something which can be definitively attained at a certain point in time. Values differ in that they represent qualities such as honesty, love, compassion or justice that we attempt to bring to each and every moment and that we endeavor to embody regardless of the specific task we are doing at any given time. The focus on doing a moral inventory, repairing damaged relationships and healing character defects presents an opportunity to learn how to move through life with a commitment to our values rather than to our addiction.

Step 4:
Made a searching and fearless moral inventory of ourselves.

To make an inventory is to take a look at what is currently in stock. We must look at our strengths and assets as well as our weaknesses and defects. We take account of what we do to ourselves as well as what we do to others. We explore how we express our love for others, as well as how we may have hurt them.

The Rabbinic term for a moral inventory is *Cheshbon Hanefesh,* literally the accounting of one's soul. Related to *Cheshbon Hanefesh* is the idea of *Zehirut*/watchfulness.[12] The concept of *Zehirut* suggests that we take our own inventory constantly, guarding our words and deeds. Initially this attitude of *Zehirut* in recovery may require us to reign in our spontaneity as we monitor ourselves, but we can reclaim it when we are back on the right path. The idea of a moral inventory relates both to your addiction and to your general moral development. The key idea in both of these areas is to keep your focus on God, not on your addiction. The inventory helps us gauge the details of our movement from a negative addiction to a more positive center.

Fundamental to the task of doing an inventory are two questions. What does God require of me? What is God's will for me? These two questions were asked frequently in the SHOFAR group. To make a *moral* inventory implies that somehow we know what is right and what is wrong. For those who come from dysfunctional or abusive families this distinction is often hard to grasp since it was taught so poorly or not at all. For example, when a child's anger is punished by a parent's own angry outbursts, what is being taught?

In Judaism the guidelines for what is right and wrong are found in the Torah and in its interpretation by the rabbis of every generation. Torah provides the basic standards against which we can judge ourselves. Care must be taken to do this process with another so that we do not judge ourselves too harshly or let ourselves off too easily. When reading the Torah it is important to consult with someone who is knowledgeable in its interpretation. I once counseled a young, spiritually minded, but not religiously observant woman who for many years after reading a commentary on the Torah felt that she was an evil person *because* she was depressed. It took several months of counseling to assure the woman that she was depressed because of the evil she had experienced and that her feelings and actions in response to that evil were well within the scope of Jewish law.

The Torah contains many *mitzvoth.* While *mitzvah* is usually translated as commandment, it also connotes guidance and connection. The *mitzvoth* are what connect us to *HaShem*. The *mitzvoth* are concerned with both rituals such as keeping kosher (the Jewish dietary laws) and keeping the many laws of the Sabbath, and with being a just and ethical person. While some traditionalists believe observance is required simply because the Torah is the Word of God, the rabbis vigorously debated the reasons for the commandments. In the Talmud we find the idea that God gave us the commandments, not for His sake, but to purify His creatures.

Earlier we spoke of the Exodus as a paradigm for addiction and recovery. The entire Torah can be seen as a story of relapse and recovery. From the patriarchs down to Moses we have a story of ancestors who struggled with dysfunctional families and with the temptations of the idolatry and immorality that surrounded them. Many of their contacts with God were about how to stay in recovery, to faithfully serve One God.

Our rabbis taught that the performance of each *mitzvah* should be accompanied by *kavannah* (intention/awareness). *Kavannah* is the glue that connects us to *HaShem*. In practice we can imagine that each of our actions and *mitzvoth* are accompanied by an arrow of awareness pointing our attention to *HaShem*. In this way the occasions calling on us to perform a *mitzvah* (e.g., saying a blessing before eating, or refusing to gossip) become opportunities to expand our awareness of how our speech, thoughts, feelings, and actions affect our relationship to our true self, to God, to others, and to the world.

Doing an inventory of the *mitzvoth* we do or don't do, and how we do them is an important aspect of our moral inventory. An inventory of your *mitzvoth* provides a general indicator of whether you are essentially moving in the direction of your Higher Power or in the direction of your addiction.

It is traditional to prepare for Passover by searching out and eliminating all leavened products in one's house. The spiritual counterpart of this is to search one's soul and eliminate all that is leavened, or puffed up and haughty, within oneself. These physical and spiritual preparations allow us to eat the Passover *matzo* as people who are truly ready to be redeemed.

As we tell the story of the Exodus it is important that we tell the story of our own exodus from slavery/addiction. We have to identify those narrow places in our lives that enslave us: our addictions, beliefs, and inappropriate character traits.

Equally important for our journey is knowing where we are going. The Promised Land of recovery is a place called Sanity. Sometimes people wander for years in the wilderness of insanity trying to escape. The essential point is to remember that the key to the Promised Land is service. Our redemption from slavery/addiction is not for the purpose of total freedom; it is for the purpose of serving God, others, and our own Highest Good. [13]

SOURCES:

1. Rabbi Pinchas ben Yair adduced that the first trait to cultivate in the perfection of service of God is watchfulness. "The idea of watchfulness is for a person to exercise caution in his actions and his undertakings; that is to deliberate and watch over his actions and his accustomed ways to determine whether or not they are good ... as our Sages of blessed memory said (Talmud, Sotah 5b), 'All who deliberate upon their paths in this world will be worthy to witness the salvation wrought by the Holy One Blessed be He.'"

    (*The Path of the Just,* chapter II, Concerning the Trait of Watchfulness[14])

2. What does *HaShem,* your God, ask of you, but that you fear *HaShem* your God, walking in all His ways, and to love Him and serve *HaShem* your God with all your heart/mind and all your soul. To observe the *mitzvoth* of *HaShem* and His enactments which I enjoin upon you this day, for your own good. ... Fear *HaShem* your God, serve Him, embrace Him, and swear by His name. (Deuteronomy 10:12, 13 and 20)

    Luzzato states that, "walking in His ways embodies the whole area of cultivation and correction of character traits."[15] Other commentators view the observance of the commandments as a means to achieve the fear of God. Most see fear of God as an essential character trait which leads us to love of God, to serve God and to follow the *mitzvoth.* Fear of God may sound like an alien concept to modern Jews who see it as distancing us from God. Fear can be seen from two different perspectives. On the one hand it can be viewed as the fear associated with reward and punishment. We fear God because we fear punishment if we do wrong. This concept of fear based on Divine retribution is unpalatable to some. A second approach to fear is from the perspective of one who has already come very close to God and fears the loss of that closeness. This fear is like that of a lover who fears the loss of a life long companion. The person in recovery is likely to fear loss of focus on his or her Higher Power because that is likely to lead to relapse and disaster.

    The idea of embracing God may be understood as having constant God awareness. This essential skill for recovery requires us to be aware of where we are directing our thoughts at each moment. We will learn how to achieve this fear and awareness of God in later steps. For now it is important that we take stock of our current status.

3.   Maimonides in his *Mishneh Torah*, Instruction on Ethical Ideas lists eleven *mitzvoth* which form the basis of ethical behavior. These are included here as examples of ethical *mitzvoth* which you can include in your inventory. [Numbers in parentheses indicate chapter and paragraph]

1. To copy His ways (1:6) Generally one who follows the middle path between extremes is a *chacham* (wise one). One who is meticulous is a *tzadik* (righteous one). God's ways include: Compassion, Mercy, Patience, Abundant Loving Kindness, Righteousness, Straight, Wholeness, Courage, Strength.
2. To cleave to those who know *HaShem* (5 & 6)
   People are drawn to the attitudes and actions of their neighbors.
   We cleave to *HaShem* by cleaving to sages. (6:2)
3. To love your neighbors (6:3; see Leviticus 19:18)
   This includes praising him and guarding his property.
4. To love the resident aliens (*gerim*), converts (6:4)
5. Not to hate brothers (6:5)
6. To reprove others (6:6)
   a) "You shall clearly reprove your neighbor." (Leviticus 19:17) If someone offends you, ask 'why did you do this to me?'
   b) Reprove anyone who sins, even two or three times, until the sinner strikes you and says "I won't listen." (6:7)
7. Not to embarrass others. Do not speak harshly in reproof. This applies to *mitzvoth* among people (*bein adam l'chavero*); but concerning *HaShem*, if the offender doesn't repent we embarrass him in public as did the prophets. (6:8)
8. Not to oppress orphans or widows (6:10)
9. Not to gossip (and slander) (7:1)
10. Not to take revenge (7:7)
11. Not to bear a grudge (7:6)

In addition to the preceding eleven *mitzvoth* the following thoughts from Maimonides are pertinent to our discussion of Step 4.

12. Each person should direct their awareness and all their deeds to knowing (to the experience of) God. ... All eating and drinking should be done not for physical pleasure alone, but rather for the healthful maintenance of the body.

13. Every action should be with thought of serving *HaShem*: work, exercise, eating, sleeping, sex; (as written in the Biblical book of Proverbs (3:6)), "In all your ways acknowledge Him (God) and he will make your paths smooth." (3:3)

14. A sage speaks gently, gives everyone a friendly greeting in order to console their spirit, judges all people favorably, loves peace and pursues it, praises, doesn't disparage others, speaks when appropriate, and speaks only about wisdom & *Gemilut Hasadim* (deeds of loving kindness). (5:7)

PROCESS: *Doing Step 4*

Here are some general considerations for doing a moral inventory / *Chesbon hanefesh*:

- The focus of the inventory should be on the present and on your addiction or other dysfunctional behavior.
- Review the past only to the extent that you are carrying it into the present and it affects your present behavior.
- Focus only on yourself: what you did, said, thought and felt; not on what others did or said.
- Four different approaches to doing a moral inventory are provided here. Try each one for a period of time before moving on to the next.

1. **A Basic Daily Inventory**

Set aside some time each day, or minimally each week, to do your inventory. It is traditional to review one's daily actions at night, when one says the *Shema Yisrael* before retiring. You can do the inventory in whatever way is most helpful to you, meditating or writing.

Some questions to provide structure for your daily inventory are

A. How did I let or not let my addiction rule me today?
B. What feelings or behaviors led me to the wrong path today?
C. What feelings and behaviors helped me today?
D. What were the defects and accomplishments in:
> How I treated myself?
> How I treated others?
> How I related to or was aware/unaware of God?

2. **Spiritual Inventory**:

After becoming familiar with doing the Basic Inventory you may try a more extensive spiritual inventory which covers the three basic areas of Jewish spirituality: God, Torah, and Israel. Write down your responses to these questions.

A. ***HaShem*/God**: Who and what am I spiritually? What thoughts do I have about myself? How do I relate to my Higher Power? What have I learned from the first three steps? Do I feel connected to my Higher Power? How does God feel about me? How do I give meaning to my life?

B. **Torah**: Have I chosen a clearly articulated moral and ethical path? Have I used my tradition as a source of strength, guidance, and meaning or do I view my tradition as a burden or irrelevant?

What have I done to learn about my tradition and to practice it? How do I use *mitzvoth* to connect me with my Higher Power?

C. **Israel**: How do I feel about being Jewish? How am I involved with other Jews? Am I involved with any group which serves as a source of support, trust, and guidance in my work of recovery and becoming a better person and Jew? What do I do to nurture and support the communities I live in? How do I show my respect for others? How often do I do favors for others? Do I do anything that might be harmful to others or the world?

3. Life Review Inventory

Another approach to step 4 is through meditation on fundamental questions of your existence. This type of inventory is focused more on the general moral direction of one's life rather than specific aspects as suggested above. The purpose of these questions is to help you prioritize your moral values. Having a clear awareness of your moral foundations can serve as an anchor when you are going through stormy times, or 'hit bottom.'

Set aside a block of time, and write about one or more of the following questions:[16] You may also try choosing one question and silently meditating on it for an extended period of time (e.g., an hour).

A. Divide your life into segments (e.g. childhood, secondary school, college, marriage, middle years, etc.) During each segment what have you done with your life? What have you accomplished? What are you proud of? What are you ashamed of? What have you given to others?

B. What values or beliefs give your life meaning?

C. What relationships (family, friends, work, etc.) are most important to you?

D. What do you want to contribute to the world during your life?

E. What do you want to get from life during your lifetime?

F. If you had your life to live over, what would you change? What would you keep the same? What would you try to accomplish?

G. For what ideals, if any, would you be willing to die?

H. What would bring you more happiness than anything else in the world or would be like heaven on earth for you?

4. Character Trait Inventory

The time between Passover and Shavuot (the *Omer* period) has been associated with a Jewish mystical tradition of self examination. Each of the forty-nine days of the *Omer* corresponds to a unique combination of character traits derived from seven essential traits or attributes (*middot*). These essential character traits are derived from seven manifestations or emanations of the Divine called *sefirot* (singular: *sefirah*). The *sefirot* may be seen as channels for the flow of Divine energy.[17] (The seven *sefirot*/character traits are described in the chart below.) Each of the seven levels contains within it aspects of all seven levels making a total of forty-nine inner aspects of the divine/human self. On each day of the Omer period Jewish mystics take up the challenge of repairing any of their character defects that are related to the specific *sefirot* corresponding to that day.

One way to do the fourth step would be to go through the *sefirot* and do an inventory of how each quality or combination of qualities is reflected in your behavior or personality. Where are you strong and where can you grow? This is most easily done when you select a specific incident with which you had difficulty. The chart below lists each of the *sefirot*, gives its basic meaning, describes the related virtues and vices of each *sefirah*, and states an inventory question for you to answer. Each week of the *Omer* (or any other time period you choose) do a daily inventory related to one of the *sefirot* using the following chart.

SEFIROT
DIVINE MANIFESTATIONS - CHARACTER TRAITS[18]

For each of the *Sefirot* the meaning of each term is given first. The corresponding virtue/vice is then given in bold faced type.

Sefirot related to feelings:

Hesed (love)   kindness, grace, unlimited flow
love / lust
Hesed refers to the feeling of an abundant, unlimited flow of love and grace. This energy can be channeled into love or lust. Did my actions flow from a true sense of love and kindness or was I simply trying to meet my own needs inappropriately?

Gevurah (restraint) might, justice, power in the sense of severity, restriction
control, justice / fear, hate
Gevurah represents restriction and control. Its purpose is to focus the energy of Hesed. Did I act out of strength and respect for my self and others or was I acting out of weakness, fear, or insecurity which I tried to conceal with anger or over-controlling behavior?

Tiferet (beauty) compassion; a balance of hesed and gevurah
compassion / indulgence
When Hesed and Gevurah are balanced the result is the affirming and healing energy of Tiferet. Unbalanced, the energy of Tiferet becomes chaos (as in addiction). Did I balance love and power? Did I express my love for myself or others in a reasonable, compassionate way, within appropriate limits, or was I overbearing or overindulgent?

Sefirot related to behavior:

Netzach (victory)   perpetuity, will power, everlastingness, (lasting recovery)
energized engagement & will power / willfulness & addiction
The energized engagement of Netzach can be directed into the willfulness of addiction or the will power of recovery. Does my behavior reflect energized engagement in recovery?

37

Hod (glory)   splendor, dignity, devotion, empathy
commitment & consistency / impulsivity & promiscuity
Hod focuses the energy of Netzach just as Gevurah   focuses and limits Hesed. Did I demonstrate my devotion to my principles and my Higher Power, repudiating temptations to relapse (people, places and things) or was I acting on impulse?   Was I consistent and disciplined?

Yesod (foundation) foundation of sexual energy, connectivity
loyalty / disconnection

Yesod reflects the balance of Netzach and Hod, an energized, dignified and optimally effective ordering of one's behavior. Was I connected to my own thoughts, feelings and actions? Was I disconnected from or unable to communicate with my own thoughts, needs and feelings? Did my actions reflect my being fully in recovery and being connected to my Higher Power? Did I set a good example?

Sefirah of total integration:

Malkhut (sovereignty)   majesty, authority
surrender & acceptance / stubbornness & rebellion
Do I live my life in full awareness of the world as an expression of my Higher Power's love? Am I engaged in positive creative actions for enhancing others, myself and the world?

Step 5:
Admitted to God, to ourselves, and to another human being the exact nature of our wrongs.

The admission or confession of our wrongs to God, to ourselves and to another is essential to understanding the exact nature of our wrongs. As long as we keep our thoughts to ourselves, our understanding about what we have done may remain clouded by our defenses. We are vulnerable to the opposing tendencies of either rationalizing away improper behavior or seeing ourselves as worse than we really are. It is only through confession and communication that we are able to gain a clear understanding of our wrongs and their impact on our self esteem.

With Step 5 we begin to explore and work through the material which we generated in Step 4. We are asked to admit not only our wrongs but "the exact nature of our wrongs" as well. This phrase implies a deeper level of self understanding, knowing not only what the errors were, but also the thoughts and emotions which generated that behavior. Often the knowledge of what was or was not wrong requires input from another source. That input might come from discussion with a friend or sponsor, or from reading.

As we will see in the sources, Judaism requires confession of wrongs before God and to oneself. While confessing our wrongs to another person is not part of the process of *teshuvah*, it may nevertheless be a practical tool.

For those who experienced abuse as a child, understanding the exact nature of one's wrong may be an especially difficult task. Sometimes we ended up feeling shame and guilt for things that really weren't wrong because our sense of reality had been distorted. Normally, when a child or adult has behaved inappropriately the awareness of guilt and feelings of shame help the person to get back on the proper path. In dysfunctional families shame and guilt are often linked to behavior for which the person cannot be held accountable in an appropriate way. Either a person feels guilt and shame for behavior which is not their own, or for behavior which really isn't wrong.[19] For example, a child may be blamed for and shamed by a parent's drunken rage. At times children may be blamed and shamed for failing to live up to unrealistically high expectations.

The result of dysfunctional shame and guilt is that the person thinks and feels that he or she is worthless, deficient, or shameful. The dysfunctional guilt and shame of abuse cannot be challenged directly so the individual often resorts to passive or indirect methods of dealing with the shame and guilt. Some examples of passive or indirect methods are social withdrawal, adapting to what others need and want at the expense of one's own needs and wants, and destructive self-expression such as addictions and compulsions. Correcting these incorrect beliefs and behaviors requires courage, patience, commitment to the recovery process and a sincere investment of time and effort.

SOURCES

> Confession of sins is part of a process which includes a resolve to turn from sin, and regret for the sin.

1. If a person has transgressed any one of the positive or negative *mitzvoth* in the Torah, whether intentionally or unintentionally, then when he repents and turns away from sin, he must confess before God, blessed is He, as it is written: "If a man or woman commits any human transgression, ... they must confess their transgressions which they have committed" (Numbers 5:6-7); this means verbal confession. How does one confess? He says: "Praise *HaShem, chatati,* I have missed the mark, I have done evil, I have rebelled against you and have done so and such .... See, I regret and am ashamed of my actions; I will never repeat this again." This represents the essential part of confession. Those who confess repeatedly and expand upon this matter are praise worthy.
   (Maimonides, *Mishneh Torah,* Laws of Repentance: 1: 1)

   > Maimonides' comments about confession clearly define it as an essential part of *teshuvah*. He links confession with regret and resolve to change. *Teshuvah* is an all encompassing process. For that reason, when we discuss one aspect of *Teshuvah,* we will often touch upon more than one Step. The phrase *confess before God* implies that this confession is an act of prayer. [20]

   > Members of the Shofar group were often troubled by the use of the term "sin" instead of "wrong." As mentioned in the Introduction to Steps 4 through 9, the Hebrew word *chet,* often translated as "sin," actually means "to miss the mark." In the next source we have an interesting comment on this concept offered by Rabbi J Soloveitchik.

2. The Hebrew verb, *hatati,* does not mean "I have sinned." It means "I have stumbled, I missed my goal; sin has failed me; sin has brought me to despair and led me astray."
   Soloveitchik On Repentance: The Thought and Oral Discourses of Rabbi Joseph B. Soloveitchik. Pinchas H. Peli. New York: Paulist Press, 1984. Page 65.

Confession of sins is found in the following prayers:

3. *ASHAMNU* /We have sinned....
   Our God and God of our ancestors, may our prayer come before You, and do not ignore our supplication for we are not so in denial and stiff necked as to say to you *HaShem*, our God and the God of our ancestors, that we are righteous and have not missed the mark, but we and our families have sinned: We have become ashamed, we have betrayed, we have stolen, we have slandered, we have caused evil (by not setting limits), we have caused wickedness, we have been willful (made our own will into a Higher Power), we have acted violently (used our words to coerce others), we have falsely charged others, we have given poor advice, we have lied, we have scorned, we have rebelled, we have acted indignantly, we have turned away, we have done evil, we have acted rebelliously, we have caused distress, we have been stiff necked, we have been wicked, we have corrupted, we have done loathsome acts, we have gone astray, we have led others astray.

   > Please note that all of these sins are listed in the plural rather than in the singular. It is clear that no one would conceivably commit all of these sins, however, we as a community list all the sins from A to Z (in Hebrew: *alef* to *tav*). We are taught that *Kol Yisrael aravim zeh bazeh* (Each of us in Israel is responsible for the other). And so we confess in the plural, acknowledging that our action or inaction may have been in part responsible for someone else's sin, even inadvertently. *Ashamnu* appears in the daily prayers and is an important part of the *Yom Kippur* liturgy.

   > In the *Shemoneh Esrei* (Eighteen blessings) week day prayer the following may be inserted in the paragraph which begins 'Hear our voice.'

4. Please, *HaShem*, I have missed the mark, I have done wrong, and willfully rebelled before You, from the day I was created until today, and especially I have missed the mark by... [here you may insert the particular sin(s) for which you seek atonement]. Please *HaShem*, for the sake of your great Name, grant me atonement for my wrongs, my errors, and my rebellious sins in which I have missed the mark, done wrong, and

willfully rebelled before You from my youth until this day. Make whole all the Names that have been blemished in Your Great Name.

The above prayer deals not only with confession but also with atonement and feelings of regret. The idea of "making whole all the Names that have been blemished in Your Great Name" requires some explanation. In Jewish mystical thought each of our actions in this plane of reality is considered to influence higher levels and aspects of reality. Along with our repairing any damage we have done in this world, we ask God to repair any damage which our actions caused in higher realms. This act of confession is clearly part of the process of *teshuvah* in which we return to God and resolve to mend our ways.

PROCESS: *Doing Step5*

1. Admit your wrongs to yourself by writing them in your journal. Talk to God about these wrongs. Talk to a friend to get perspective.

_____

_____

_____

_____

_____

_____

_____

_____

_____

_____

_____

_____

_____

_____

_____

_____

_____

2. Use the prayer cited in Source 4 above or compose your own prayer of confession to do Step 5.

_____

_____

_____

_____

_____

_____

_____

_____

_____

_____

_____

_____

_____

_____

_____

_____

_____

3. In exploring the exact nature of our wrongs it is often helpful to understand that the various thoughts, feelings and impulses that we experience sometimes reflect certain thinking errors. These errors may be based on automatic patterns of thinking that we learned early in our lives. Thinking errors include the following mistakes:

    1. All-or Nothing Thinking - a tendency to see everything in black and white terms with no shades of gray.
    2. Catastrophizing - imagining that the worst possible consequences will occur.
    3. Emotional Reasoning - a tendency to rationalize our thinking based on how we feel. "I feel it, therefore it must be true."
    4. "Should" Statements - ideas that we or others have told us about how we should or ought to be. e.g.: I should be perfect. I should be strong. I should not show feelings.
    5. Personalization - imagining that a situation or someone else's speech or behavior actually affects your self worth when it is only an external event or someone else's reaction to you. [21]

Whenever you feel as though you have done something wrong ask yourself if you have made a thinking error. If you have, one possible way to respond is to think of a rational response which you can make to refute your mistaken belief. Think about what you might say to someone else who was in a similar situation. There is an alternative approach you may use, especially if you can not think of a rational response, or if you can not shake a pervasive feeling that something is wrong with you (as opposed to having done one bad thing). Notice that you are having a negative thought about yourself and label it. Say to yourself 'there is that negative self talk again,' or 'I am having the thought that ….'" Notice the thought simply as a thought and not necessarily as a fact. Then begin to take some action that you know will move you in the direction of your recovery.

It is improper to confess and regret sins which we did not really commit, but are only products of our own distorted thinking. However, if you cannot identify a thinking error and you have clearly committed some wrong it is certainly appropriate to admit that and proceed with the process of *teshuvah.*

STEPS 6 and 7

Were entirely ready to have God remove all these defects of character. Humbly asked Her to remove our shortcomings

At first glance Steps 6 and 7 seem to assume that we cannot change on our own. The emphasis appears to be on God as the shaper and mender of our character. While we may wish that God would remove our shortcomings, the actual burden of these steps is on us. We must make ourselves ready and humbly ask for what we desire.

Being ready to have all defects of character removed entails:

- a readiness to take total responsibility for all of one's actions,
- a total willingness to stand humbly before God recognizing that our soul and body are God's creations. (see steps 1 & 2),
- a readiness to live with the truth that you are created in the image of God and have free will,
- fully turning to God through *teshuvah* / doing the 12 steps. (see sources), and
- being clear about what we no longer want to be, as well as knowing what we value and want to become.

Steps 6 and 7 can be extremely intimidating especially when we have the idea that we actually are our character. Character is an aspect of self that develops and changes through life. Many people are familiar with the popular idea that various experiences (e.g., hard work, pain, suffering) build good character. Implicit in this idea is the notion that character is acquired and can be altered. It is not the essence of who we are. From a spiritual point of view the soul represents the essence of the human being. We can "clothe" the soul in the "garments" of our thoughts, speech and actions. The garments of the soul are soiled when we are active in our addiction. Fortunately, with help from our Higher Power we can remove the soiled garments. The positive thoughts, speech and actions that we can perform replace the soiled garments with clean ones.

Participants in most 12 step meetings are encouraged to introduce themselves with the phrase, "Hi, I'm Mike and I'm an addict (alcoholic, drug user, over eater, etc.). Identifying oneself as an addict is actually useful in the early stages of recovery as it helps to cut through the denial which is so often a part of addiction. It should be clear, however, that this identification is simply another way of conceptualizing who you are. Like all other concepts of self we must understand that this is just an abstraction and not a statement of who we essentially are. We have the experience of engaging in addictive thinking, feeling and behavior, but we are not the addiction. The idea of the "addict" is a conceptualization of self or a garment of the soul that we are in the process of discarding and replacing with a new more functional concept or clean garment.

When we strongly identify with our concept of who we are we may believe that change is impossible. Thoughts that we are an addict, that we are evil, that we are failures, that we are worthless and similar negative thoughts become difficult to remove when we actually believe that we are the thought and that the thought is a fact. The reality is that thoughts and feelings are experiences that we have. You do not have the same thoughts and feelings at age 50 as you had at age 25. You do not have the same thoughts and feelings at age 25 as you had at age 5. As you grow through life your thoughts, feelings and abilities change. The constant throughout life is not the "conceptual self," but the "observer self" or soul that is present to witness and have all of these experiences. [21]

When we are willing to let go of all of the ever changing concepts of who we are and simply experience our basic self or soul as it exists in the moment we are in touch with the part of the self that is a reflection of our Higher Power. Turning to the soul and Higher Power within holds the potential for tremendous personal transformation. Humbly standing before our Higher Power presents us with the opportunity to reshape our lives. In this place of humility and spiritual power we can see through and discard all of the falsehood and deception that was part of our addiction. In this place of life and renewal we can let go of the distorted concepts of self and negative character traits that we have accumulated like so many soiled rags that we had falsely taken to be the only garments that we could wear. From this place we can begin to rebuild our lives with our Higher Power at the center, and our highest values surrounding and guiding us.

Knowing what kind of person we want to become requires a readiness and willingness to study our tradition in order to learn what God's will is and what the positive character traits are that we need to develop. Your preparation for this step will be greatly enhanced by having completed Steps 4 and 5.

Selecting and setting our sights on what we want is only the beginning. We must then take concrete steps to help ourselves remove our shortcomings. Such concrete actions will truly demonstrate our readiness to change and our humility in asking for God's help. Practical strategies for using our goals as tools for personal transformation will be presented below in the Process Section of this step.

SOURCES:

1.   (1) A Psalm of David

             (2) Be gracious to me, God,
                     according to your loving kindness
                     As in keeping with Your abundant mercy
                     blot out my transgressions.

             (3) Wash me thoroughly of my iniquity,
                     and from my sin purify me,
                     for I recognize my transgressions,
                     and my missing of the mark is always before me.

             (4) Against You alone have I sinned (missed the mark),
                     and I have done what is evil in Your sight;
                     so that You are justified when you speak,
                     and correct in Your judgment.

             (11) Hide Your face from my sins;
                     and all my evil doings blot out.

             (12) A pure heart create for me, God;
                     and a correct spirit renew within me.

             (13) Do not cast me away from Your Presence,
                     and do not take Your Holy Spirit from me.

             (14) Return to me the joy of your salvation,
                     let a generous spirit sustain me.

             (15) I will teach transgressors Your ways,
                     so that those who miss the mark will return to You.

Psalm 51 reflects the themes which we find in these and other steps. As you read it identify the steps which mirror the theme(s) of each verse. Notice the great humility of the psalmist, his admission of guilt, his request for purification, and his goals.

2. For the virtue of this day (*Yom Kippur*) will acquit you to cleanse you, from all your sins before *HaShem* you will be cleansed.[22] (Leviticus 16:30)

> The *Torah* tells us that we can repent of our sins, that our sincere prayers will be accepted by God, and that forgiveness will be granted. Yes, you really can change. This verse from Leviticus indicates that God has given us a gift, the Day of Atonement. Through the virtue of this day, which we spend in prayer and repentance, forgiveness is granted to us for all of our sins against God.

3. Bring us back our Father, to Your *Torah*, and bring us near, our King, to Your service, and aid us in returning in perfect repentance (*teshuvah*) before You. Blessed are You *HaShem*, Who desires repentance.

Forgive us, our Father, for we have missed the mark; pardon us our King, for we have willfully sinned; for You pardon and forgive. Blessed are You *HaShem*, the gracious One Who pardons abundantly.

> These blessings, the fifth and sixth blessings of the daily *Shemoneh Esrei* prayer are related to steps 6 and 7 and to the themes of repentance and forgiveness. Again, we are taught that God desires our repentance and freely grants pardon for all of our transgressions.

4. As mentioned above, *teshuvah*, fully turning to God, is required as part of our preparation for step 6. Maimonides in his great work on Jewish law *The Mishneh Torah* gives a clear account of what is required for *teshuvah* as well as important reflections on the process. The following is excerpted from his "Laws of Repentance". [Numbers refer to chapter and law.]

(2:2): *Teshuvah* is when the sinner
a) abandons his/her sin
b) removes it from his/her thoughts
c) resolves in his/her heart/mind not to do it again
d) regrets the transgression
e) confesses in words.

(5:1): Free will is granted to every human being. If a person wishes to follow a good path and be righteous, he is able to do so; if he wishes to follow the evil path and be wicked, he is able to do so. It is written: "So, man has become like one of us, knowing good and evil." (Genesis 3:22)

> The concept of free will teaches us that if we want our defects of character removed, the first step in doing so is making a decision to choose the path of life. Our future may be influenced by our past, but it is not entirely determined by it. We can change and get into recovery at any moment.

(5:4): Do not wonder, saying: 'How can a person do all that he desires and have all of his actions under his control? Is there anything in the world that can be done without his Creator's authority and against God's wish?' -- Know, indeed, that God performs everything according to His desire, even though our actions are under our own control.

> Maimonides statement reveals a deep truth to us. Even though God is the ultimate source of everything that happens, we are still in control of ourselves and our actions. If everything was predetermined then the statements of the Torah enjoining us to act ethically would be meaningless. When we take a spiritual path we often find paradox, not simple answers. It is important to know that one can achieve peace of mind by coming to terms with paradox, rather than attempting to resolve or eliminate the paradox with simplistic answers.

(7:4): The person who has successfully turned to *HaShem* should not imagine that he is far removed from the level of the righteous because of the evil and mistakes he has committed. This is not so. He is dearly loved by the Creator as if he had never sinned. Additionally, his reward is great, since he has tasted sin, removed himself from it, and conquered his evil impulse.

PROCESS: *Doing Steps 6 & 7*

1.   Review the work you have done in Steps 4 and 5. Be certain that you understand the exact nature of your wrongs and that you are clear about how you would like to change. Then recite Psalm 51 (see sources) as preparation for doing the work of these steps.

2.   Select one of defects which you identified in Steps 4 and 5. Have a talk with God. Ask God to help you learn to deal with the problems which confront you, to meet your needs in appropriate ways, and to discover how to remove obstacles to recovery.

3.   The following imagery exercise (HEART) is a tool you may use to take a more active role in removing defects of character and other shortcomings.

HEART

Relax...   Get comfortable... Close your eyes...   Take three slow breaths, taking longer to exhale than to inhale...

Select one of the defects you wish to correct. Perhaps focus on your addiction itself.

Imagine yourself going through a situation or scenario in which the defect or addiction has become evident again. See yourself at the point in time where you first begin to notice the urge to act or the urge to indulge your addiction....

Imagine a HEART with a brightly flashing arrow pointing you in the direction of God. ...

Explore your current experience.....   Open your awareness to whatever sensations, feelings or thoughts the addictive urge may be covering up. (Perhaps it is a feeling of rejection, unworthiness, being unloved, failure, shame, guilt or some other negative feeling.) ...

Let yourself know that having a variety of negative thoughts and feelings is a common experience. Thoughts and feelings constantly come and go in the mind and you can have them without acting on them.

Remind yourself that you are created in God's image.....   Your decision to turn your life and your will over to your Higher Power means that you must satisfy your needs or express your feelings in appropriate ways....

Now see yourself doing what you know is right, correcting your defect.... As you imagine the situation, be aware of any hesitation, fear or anxiety. If you wish you may enter into that feeling and explore it....

Look for the source of the fear or problem.... Identify what you need to do or say to yourself to overcome your fear or hesitation.

Are you ready to be the new Person you imagined?

If you aren't ready, take some time to meditate on what you need to do next.

If you experience any hesitation, fear or anxiety, talk to that part of yourself....
Let yourself know again that you are created in God's image as a loving, powerful, balanced individual....

If you are ready to be a new person, again imagine yourself going through the situation from start to finish doing what you know is appropriate....

Experience the positive feelings of peace or satisfaction which come from turning to the right path, knowing that your prayer has been answered and that you have the inner resources to overcome any defect in character....

As you experience this peace and satisfaction say *"BARUCH HASHEM,"* "Blessed and acknowledged is My Higher Power." Know that any time you begin to feel the urge to repeat your character defect all you need to do is say *BARUCH HASHEM* to remember the positive feelings which come from taking alternative action and to know that your Higher Power will help you to find the best path for you.

Take 3 more deep breaths.

Say to yourself *BARUCH HASHEM.*

Open your eyes.

The imagery described above should be rehearsed regularly. In order to facilitate that process you can use the HEART tool which reviews the essential points of the imagery using the letters of HEART as a guide. A one page guide to using HEART will be found in the appendix to this book. To make optimal use of HEART please continue to work on the next process suggestion related to making positive affirmations.

5. Go back to the chart of the *Sefirot* in Step 4. Look over the inventory which you did then. Make an affirmation for yourself related to each *Sefirah* or area which you feel is in need of improvement. The following suggestions might serve as the beginning of your list.

Hesed *I am full of love and kindness. I feel myself being filled with an abundant flow of Divine love.*

Gevurah *I have the strength to act respectfully and justly towards my self and others. I feel myself filled with an abundant flow of Divine strength and discipline.*

Tiferet *I balance love and justice, kindness and power, and set reasonable limits. I see the flow of hesed and gevurah energies creating a Divinely balanced state of Tiferet/healing in my body and spirit.*

Netzach *I am energized to achieve as much as I can and to take frequent action to enhance my recovery. I feel myself being filled with the energy to act.*

Hod *I demonstrate my devotion to my recovery, my principles and my Higher Power. I feel myself filled with dignity.*

Yesod   *I am energetically and mindfully connected to my own thoughts, feelings and actions, to others, and to my Higher Power with true dignity regardless of where I am or what I am doing.*

Malkhut   *I live my life in full awareness of the world as an expression of my Higher Power's love. I am engaged in positive creative actions for enhancing others, myself and the world.*

There are several ways to do affirmations. You can look in a mirror and say the affirmation aloud to yourself several times every morning and evening. Use the affirmations above or create your own positive affirmations of who you want to be.

You can also spend fifteen or twenty minutes meditating on a single affirmation, exploring all aspects of the affirmation and seeing how it can be manifest in all areas of your life. As you meditate be aware of any mental or emotional blocks you encounter, any unusual sensations in your body, or ways in which you alter the affirmation/meditation. Use your awareness as a guide to explore areas you need to change or to which you should pay special attention.

.

STEPS 8 and 9:
Made a list of all persons we had harmed, and became willing to make amends to them. Made direct amends to such people where ever possible, except when to do so would injure them or others.

Making amends is an integral part of *teshuvah*. Admitting that you have done wrong is often the first step in making amends. It demonstrates that you are willing to take responsibility for what you have done. Amends, repayment, and confession are all elements needed for forgiveness.

In relationships amends are important, but it is often hard to figure out how to make amends in a practical sense. For example, how do you make amends for anger, rage, or emotional abuse? It is certainly not as simple as repaying money which has been stolen. The process begins with apology, admitting what one has done, expressing regret, and being willing to be responsible for one's thoughts, feelings, and behavior. All of these actions are necessary to achieve atonement (*kapparah*) and forgiveness.

Real healing in a relationship requires even more - a complete change of oneself in which the anger or other character defect is conquered and overcome. This process of complete change is referred to as *taharah* or purification.[23] Learning to respond and live in new ways you are re-created as a new person.

Willingness to make amends may be difficult to achieve if you still feel anger and hostility or have not done steps 6 and 7. If you find it hard to make amends go back and do steps 5 through 7 again.

Make amends to yourself. It is often hard to identify ways in which you have wronged yourself. Figuring out how to make amends to yourself is hard, too. We want to treat ourselves with respect and joy without overindulgence. Rabbi Twersky's teaching on leisure is an instructive example: You need a good balance of leisure to refresh yourself, to do work, and to serve *HASHEM*, but too much leisure becomes self-indulgence.[24]

In the process of making amends we also must deal with the issue of forgiveness. Often we have wronged the same individual who has acted poorly towards us. Accepting forgiveness from another is often much easier than forgiving when you have been wronged. We have learned that God forgives our wrongs when we engage in the process of *teshuvah*. In the sources that follow we will see that it is equally good to offer forgiveness to those who have wronged us and approach us in the spirit of *teshuvah*.

Forgiving does not imply that we will forget what was done or that we condone wrong doing. It does mean that we have come to a place of healing and wholeness in ourselves that enables us to accept the humanity and the amends of the one who has offended us. Forgiving involves accepting that what was done, right or wrong, is now part of the past and that the only way for you to move on is to let go of the anger and focus your energy on becoming the recovered person that you want to be.

SOURCES: *Doing Steps 8 & 9*

1. From Maimonides, *Mishneh Torah*, Laws of Repentance.
    (2:9)   Repentance and *Yom Kippur* provide atonement only for sins committed against God, for example, when one has eaten forbidden food or committed a forbidden action, etc. However, sins committed against another person, such as when one injures, curses or robs another, are not pardoned until he compensates his neighbor and makes amends. Even though he has returned money to the offended party, he must appease the injured person and ask for his pardon. Even if he only annoyed him with words he must appease him and return to him until he is pardoned. If his fellow doesn't want to pardon him, he brings to him a panel of three of his peers, who approach him, and seek (forgiveness) from him. If it (the apology) isn't accepted from them, he repeats this procedure a second and a third time. If the apology is not accepted, he lets go of the matter and moves on. The one who refused to pardon is now the one who has missed the mark.
    (2:10) It is forbidden to be cruel by not accepting an apology; one should be easily pacified, and difficult to anger. When an offender asks for pardon, one should forgive with a whole heart and with a willing spirit. Even if he vexed him and greatly sinned against him, he must not take revenge and he must not bear a grudge.
    (2:11)   One who sins against his fellow who then dies before he seeks pardon, brings 10 people to his grave (of the offended party) and says before them, "I have sinned before *HaShem*, the God of Israel and against this person, so and so have I done to him." If he owed him money he pays it to his descendants. If he doesn't know the descendants he deposits it with a Bet Din (rabbinic court) and makes confession.

PROCESS:

The following exercise may be done individually or in a group. It is designed to help you work through steps 8 and 9. Use it to increase your motivation to do these steps and to anticipate any problems you may encounter.

Relax, close your eyes......

Go over these steps in your mind. Picture one of the people to whom you will make amends in your mind... Picture what it will be like to make amends... What will you say and do? ... How will you feel? ...

Record your reflections below. Share your imagined experience with the group. You may share what you said and did, or simply how it felt. If you need help with this process ask the group for what you need.

_____
_____
_____
_____
_____
_____
_____
_____
_____
_____
_____

STEP 10:
Continued to take personal inventory and when we were wrong promptly admitted it.

As was stated in step 4, taking a personal inventory is an ongoing process. Being well into our program of recovery, having made an inventory, admitted our wrongs, and made amends where appropriate, we are prepared to live a new a spiritual life. We cannot, however, let down our guard. Continued recovery on the path of spirituality requires constant vigilance and zeal. It is in this spirit that we examine our thoughts, feelings and actions continuously.

In Step 4 you completed a comprehensive inventory. That work should serve as a baseline against which can periodically measure your progress. At an absolute minimum you could review your inventory every year during the Ten Days of Repentance between *Rosh HaShanah* and *Yom Kippur*. It will also be beneficial to set up a fixed time daily or weekly to review your actions and progress. One traditional format for doing this work is provided in the Process section of this chapter.

Our moral inventory does not take place in a vacuum, but rather in the context of our values and expectations for ourselves. For millennia Jews have found their highest values and expectations articulated in the Torah, and expanded and explained in the Talmud and other rabbinic writings. Today, the role of the rabbi is to continue the elaboration of the traditions of the Torah in ways which render them personally meaningful, ethically relevant and economically feasible.[25]

Torah in its broadest sense is the moral and ethical standard we use as the basis for our inventory. Because it is the foundation of our spirituality and an excellent reference point for our inventory it is important to set aside regular time for Torah study. There are numerous books and web sites devoted to the entire spectrum of Torah study. Shamash - The Jewish Network lists over 5000 links on its website at http://shamash.org/. There you will find everything from introductory courses to advance study opportunities. Additional printed resources will be found in the For Further Study section at the end of this book.

SOURCES

1. Hillel used to say: 'If I am not for myself, who will be for me? If I am
    only for myself, what am I? and if not now, when?'   Shammai used to
    say, 'make your study of Torah a regular practice, say little and do much,
    and receive everyone with a cheerful face.'
    (*Ethics of the Fathers*, 1:14, 15)

    Hillel's aphorism requires careful study. As we continue to
    take inventory, questions related to the issues of
    codependency are certain to arise. "Am I doing this just to
    please others? Am I being selfish? When do I get to do
    something for me?" The message of Hillel is that we must
    constantly strive to balance two opposing tendencies: the need
    to take care of and act assertively on our own behalf, and the
    need to care for others.

    Unfortunately, there is no simple way to resolve this issue.
    However, there are some things we can do to make the task
    manageable. First and foremost we must be aware of our own
    patterns of codependency. Do you typically try to be in
    control of everything? Are you doing things for others that
    they should be doing for themselves? Are you fixing things
    that do not need to be fixed? If you find that your need to
    control is being triggered or that you are doing things for
    people without giving them a choice in the matter, beware of
    codependency.

    Please remember that it is not the specific action which is of
    concern. It is your pattern of control or your pattern of truly
    extending yourself in the service of others which you should
    continually evaluate. Codependency grows out of feelings of
    weakness and denial. True service comes from a place of
    growth and strength. When you have trouble distinguishing
    between these two tendencies seek the counsel of a sponsor,
    therapist or rabbi.

    For more information on codependency see the section in the
    appendix titled "Codependency: A Spiritual Struggle."

PROCESS: *Doing Step 10*

The traditional time for taking a personal inventory is in the evening before bedtime. We examine each day, looking at the thoughts we had, the feelings we experienced, the words we spoke and the deeds we performed. We can examine how we treated ourselves and how we interacted with others. If necessary we resolve to change our ways, make necessary amends, seek forgiveness for our wrongs and grant forgiveness to anyone who has wronged us.

Guiding us in this process are the prayers of the *K'riat Shema al Ha'mita* - the bedtime Shema. The first paragraph concerns itself with helping us cultivate the quality of forgiveness. If it is hard for you to read this paragraph, turn to page 37 and review the inventory questions suggested for the attribute of *hesed*/loving kindness. (Also see the material on forgiveness in Steps 8-9.) The second paragraph invites us to review our behavior for the day and seek forgiveness and the power to correct our errors. The final paragraph is a petition for a night of peaceful sleep. A free translation of these prayers follows:

> Master of the Universe, I now forgive anyone who has angered or provoked me or who has sinned against me, whether against my body, my property, my honor, or anything of mine, whether accidentally or intentionally, whether by word, deed, thought, or fantasy, whether in this life cycle or another. I forgive my fellow souls. Let no one be punished on my account.

> May it be your will *HaShem*, my God and God of my ancestors, that I sin no more; and those wrongs which I have committed before You today (*you may review these wrongs in some detail now*), blot out in Your abundant mercy, but not by suffering or illness. May the words of my mouth and the meditations of my heart be acceptable to You *HaShem*, my Rock and My Redeemer.

> Blessed are You *HaShem*, our God, Source of all life who brings the bonds of sleep to my eyes and slumber to my eyelids. May it be Your Will *HaShem*, my God and God of my ancestors that you help me to retire in peace and center me for peace. May my ideas, bad dreams, and strange fantasies not disturb me; may my comportment be

perfect and wholesome before you. May you enlighten my eyes lest I sleep forever, for You are the One who enlightens the eye. Acknowledged are You, *HaShem*, who illuminates the whole universe in His glory.

SHEMA YISRAEL *HASHEM* ELOKENU, *HASHEM* ECHOD.

Listen Israel, *HaShem* is our Higher Power, *HaShem* alone.

STEP 11
Sought through prayer and meditation to improve our conscious contact with God, as we understood Him, praying only for knowledge of His will for us and the power to carry that out.

Step 11 suggests that there are at least two means (prayer and meditation) with which we can achieve the goals of a) contact with God, b) knowledge of His will, and c) the power to implement His will. These goals are closely related to what Alan Mintz calls the three tasks of prayer: personal integration, access to the experience of mystery and transcendence, and the awareness of sin[26]. Jewish prayer helps us achieve these goals in specific ways as we will describe below.

Prayer and meditation are closely related but not identical. Prayer may follow a set liturgy or be a free form conversation with God. There are prayers of praise, petition and thanksgiving. The rabbis of the Talmud struggled with whether prayer ought to be fixed or spontaneous. They recognized that while a fixed liturgy could enable Jews to pray together and share common values, it could also degenerate into a meaningless, repetitive exercise. To combat this problem it was suggested that although we are provided with a standard prayer text we must add something new to our prayers each day.

To accomplish the task of adding something new to a standardized prayer, the prayer must become a meditation. Meditation is simply thinking in a focused and controlled manner. One decides to direct one's thoughts in a specific direction (to a thought, verse, object) for a specific amount of time.

To make our prayer a meditation means that we must enter into the spirit of the words and make the experiences which those words reflect come alive for us. For example, in the previous step (10) we presented a *berachah* (blessing) which is recited upon retiring in the evening. The text provides an opportunity for us to meditate on the experience of sleep, its benefits (rest and peace), and its dangers (bad dreams, fear of death). The heightened awareness generated by this meditation is then linked to our intention to bless or acknowledge our Higher Power using the words of blessing that are part of the prayer.

Similarly, any experience that evokes a feeling of awe and gratitude in us has the potential to help us to increase our conscious contact with God. To actualize this potential we are required to exercise our awareness and our intention. First we must be mindfully aware of the thoughts, emotions and sensations that comprise our experience. Then we set our intention to recognize the Presence of Our Higher Power in whatever our present experience is. We have discussed this concept earlier in the context of using blessings as a means of turning our lives over to our Higher Power.

Unfortunately, addiction often serves as a means to block out our own unpleasant experiences, thoughts and emotions. Along with the unpleasant aspects of experience we often lose contact with the pleasant aspects. Meditation is an important tool to help us regain the ability to be aware of and tolerate our own unpleasant and pleasant sensations, thoughts and emotions. Mindfulness meditation, also known as insight meditation, involves training in sustained concentration and directing attention to various aspects of personal experience. These skills are important not only for increasing our conscious contact with God, but also for helping us to understand and work with the impulses and compulsions that feed our addiction. The process of mindfulness meditation involves learning to see our thoughts, feelings and actions as experiences that the soul/self is having so that we can gain a clearer view of who we really are.

Sitting at a breakfast table after morning prayers in the synagogue one day I overheard a middle aged gentleman ask his friend, "Why do we need all these prayers? Isn't my feeling of appreciation to God enough?" I joined in the conversation responding to what was a frequently asked question in the SHOFAR group. The Bible does not specify the exact prayer formulations which we find in our prayer books, although we are bidden to thank God for the bounty He has provided us. The rabbis, since the time of Ezra the Scribe, have formulated and enacted numerous blessings and prayers with the goal of helping us deepen our relationships to God, Torah and Israel.

The basic form of the blessing, 'Blessed are You *HaShem*, our God, Sovereign of the Universe ....' conveys a number of concepts. We address God as You, denoting a very personal relationship. Speaking of God as Sovereign of the Universe conveys a sense of God's transcendence. Many of the blessings we say make mention of Israel, Jerusalem, and Torah, as well as God. The intent of the rabbis was to enfold us in a network of value concepts so that a sense of spirituality tying us to God, Torah and Israel would be constantly accessible to all.[27] As we noted earlier, Jewish spirituality does not exist solely within the confines of a personal relationship to God, but entails community and ethics as well.

Jewish prayer may be seen as a meditative reflection by which we measure ourselves against the standard of the Torah. The Hebrew word for prayer -*l'hitpalel*- is a reflexive verb which literally means 'to judge oneself.' In Judaism we not only pray for knowledge of God's will for us, but we discover God's will through the study of Torah, Talmud, Midrash, and other rabbinic literature. Sometimes what we study is unclear or even contradictory. Such problems are great opportunities for discussion with your friends or a rabbi. The meaning of "Israel" is "the one who struggles with God". When we seek to know God's will we may sometimes be disappointed that there are no easy answers to be found. The path of spirituality often leads to paradox rather than to peace of mind. As we struggles with paradox it is important to know that we are not alone, that we are part of a community of spiritual seekers who can rely on each other for love and support. We carry out God's will in the context of our families and our community. Don't forget that life and spirituality are with people as much as with God.

What does God require of me? What is God's will for me? These two questions were often asked in our group. Many of the *mitzvoth* (commandments) seem to be concerned more with rituals, such as keeping kosher (the Jewish dietary laws) and keeping the many laws of the Sabbath, than with being a just and ethical person. While some traditionalists require observance simply because the Torah is the Word/Will of God, the rabbis vigorously debated the reasons for the commandments.

In the Talmud we find the idea that God gave us the commandments, not for His sake, but to purify His creatures. I have maintained that we serve God by doing everything we do with complete attention to how our speech, thoughts, feelings, and behaviors affect our relationship to our true self, to God, to others, and to the world. (see Step 4.) *Berachot* (blessings) serve the purpose of focusing our attention on specific aspects of creation and on our relationship to the Divine Source of All. In Hasidic thought we find that one of the purposes of *mitzvoth* is to give us the opportunity to raise back to God the Holy Sparks which are hidden in the material world. This raising of the Holy Sparks is accomplished through doing *mitzvoth* with awareness and cleansing the soul.

What if we don't succeed in raising the sparks, in purifying ourselves and the world? We learn "You are not obliged to complete the work, but neither are you free to desist from beginning it."[28]

In the Passover *Hagaddah* we are told "in every generation each Jew is obligated to see him or her self as though he/she had gone out of Egypt." Just as we can never forget Egypt, we cannot forget the narrow places which imprison us, our addiction, the threat of relapse and the constant quest for recovery. We stay in recovery only when we keep our Higher Power constantly in mind. In Judaism we have built in reminders called *mitzvoth* to help us maintain our focus. In every aspect of life *mitzvoth* call us to pray, meditate and establish conscious contact with God. Traditionally three *mitzvoth* which served this function were *tzitzit, tefillin* and *mezuzah.*

The *tzitzit* were regal, knotted strings attached to one's four cornered garment. They were specifically intended to help us with impulse control. The Torah states "It will be for you a *tzitzit*, so look at it and remember all the commandments of (connectors to) God; do them (utilize them) so that you do not turn after your heart-minds and after your eyes which you whore after. So that you will remember, and do (utilize) all of My *mitzvoth* so that you will be holy to (in recovery with) your God."[29] Today traditional men wear under their shirt a small four corned garment with *tzitzit* attached. The large *tallit* (prayer shawl) is worn by men in all denominations during prayer and by women in the non-orthodox denominations.

The *Tefillin* are small leather boxes containing scriptural excerpts which are bound on the arm and on the forehead. The *Mezuzah* which contains similar scriptural portions is affixed to the door post of the house. These ritual articles are encountered regularly in traditional Jewish homes and serve as constant reminders that we should turn our thoughts to God.

There are *mitzvoth* and corresponding blessings connected with practically everything that humans do, from rising in the morning to eating, dressing, traveling, and all of life's major transitions. Through these *mitzvoth* we are constantly able to find a practical means of connecting with God and renewing our recovery.

SOURCES:

1. Just as blessings are recited over enjoyment of food or drink, so must we recite a blessing before performing every *mitzvah*. The sages instituted many blessings in the form of praise, thanksgiving and petition so that we would have the Creator (Higher Power) constantly in mind, even when not partaking of food and drink or doing a *mitzvah*.
    (Maimonides; *Mishneh Torah*, Laws of blessings, 1:3)

    There are three types of *berachot* (blessings or acknowledgements): for enjoyment, for performing a *mitzvah* and for praise (including praise, thanksgiving and petition). All three serve to help us constantly remember our Higher Power/Creator.

2. All blessings may be recited in any language, provided that they are in the form instituted by the sages. If one changes the form, the *mitzvah* is fulfilled, as long as the divine name and sovereignty as well as the subject matter of the blessing have been mentioned.
    (Maimonides; *Mishneh Torah*, Laws of blessings, 1:4.)

    This paragraph informs us that a "kosher" blessing must contain God's name and the idea that He/She is our sovereign/Higher Power. The idea that there is a specific name for our Higher Power gives us a personal connection to God and a familiar means for helping us refocus our energy on the positive when we are tempted by our addiction.

3. Rabbi Shimon says: Be meticulous in the reading of the Shema and in prayer (specifically, the *Shemoneh Esrei/Amidah* - 18 Blessings/Standing Prayer). When you pray, do not make your prayer a fixed routine, rather, (seek and experience) compassion (mercy) and grace (supplication) before God, as it is said, "For He is gracious and merciful, slow to anger, abundant in kindness, and reconcilable concerning evil;" (Joel 2:13) and do not see yourself as an evil person.
    (*Ethics of the Fathers*, 2:18)

    The issue of fixed and spontaneous prayer was addressed earlier in this chapter. The end of Rabbi Shimon's aphorism tells us that having positive self esteem is a *mitzvah*! Self esteem must, of course, be balanced with humility.

4. God compressed His will and wisdom into the 613 commandments of the Torah and their laws ... in order that each level of soul in the human body will be able to grasp them with its intellect, and in order that it (the soul) fulfill them, as far as they can be fulfilled, in action, speech and thought...
   (*Tanya*, chapter 4)

   The *Tanya* is the work of the Hasidic master Rabbi Schneur Zalman of Liadi (1745-1812), founder of the Lubovitcher branch of Hasidism. The idea expressed here is that by studying the Torah and doing *mitzvot* we are learning what God's will is for us and giving it expression in this world. *Tanya* expresses the idea of God's will in clearly mystical and supernatural terms. A more naturalistic approach to understanding God's will can be found in the contemporary writing of Rabbi Dr. Arthur Green. An excerpt from his work follows.

5. I do see a divine intent or will in the life force, as manifest in the evolutionary process, and especially in the ongoing striving towards consciousness. This is not "will" in our highly personalistic human sense, but a striving inherent in the very existence and evolution of the universe. Our human response to (or participation in!) this will is to be found in the affirmation of life, in recognizing the divine image in ourselves and in others, in acts of kindness ... and in the nurturing of awareness. ... religion is *our human fulfillment of the divine will or purpose.* (Emphasis in the original.)
   (Arthur Green, *Seek My Face, Speak My Name.* pp. 127-128)

PROCESS: *Doing Step 11*

1. If you have never meditated before learn how to do the Relaxation Response. This is a basic meditation technique common to most religious traditions. Instructions for doing the Relaxation Response are found in the appendix.

2. Select one *mitzvah*, one area of concern, a verse from the psalms, or a verse from Torah, and read it over thoroughly. Think about it and relate it to your own life. Spend some time each day for a week exploring how you can utilize this teaching in your life. As you study Torah and Jewish prayer don't feel that you must learn or say everything. Take things one piece at a time, meditating on each piece, studying, and asking questions.

3. After you have thoroughly explored an idea (see 2 above) repeat it every day like a mantra. Some teachings that you might reflect on have been included in the Sources section of this and preceding steps. A few other relevant teachings include:
    >   Serve God in happiness. (Psalm 100)
    >   Love your neighbor as yourself. (Leviticus 19:18)
    >   Know *HaShem* in all your ways. (Proverbs 6:3)
    >   In God's image you are created. (based on Genesis 1:26)
    >   Know that *HaShem* is God (your Higher Power)…. (Psalm 100:3)

4. The following meditation, taken from rabbinic legend, is traditionally said before going to sleep or before going on long voyages - times of increased vulnerability. It may be used as often as needed and is especially recommended when in need of additional power, support and help to prevent relapse. *Michael, Gabriel, Uriel*, and *Rephael* are the names of God's messengers/angels, each with a specific mission. Before using it in its entirety, meditate on each part separately. For a more elaborate version of this meditation which incorporates the 12 steps see "The Spiritual Boundary Meditation" in the last chapter of this book (More Tools for Recovery).
    >   In the name of *HASHEM*, the God of Israel,
    >   at my right - *Michael*   - who is like God in love and support
    >   at my left - *Gabriel*   - God is my strength
    >   before me - *Uriel*   - God is my light

71

behind me - *Rephael* - God is my source of healing
and above my head - *Shechinat El* - God's presence.

You will find this prayer as part of the Recitation of the *Shema* at bedtime in any traditional prayer book.

5. The affirmations based on the *sefirot* found in step 6 and 7 can be used as meditations for increasing your contact with your Higher Power. (see the Process section of those steps, tool number 4)   As you meditate on each *sefirah* you can do so with the awareness that the energy of that *sefirah* ultimately comes to you from God.

STEP 12:
Having had a spiritual awakening as the result of these steps, we tried to carry this message to anyone with an addiction and to practice these principles in all our affairs.

Step 12 tells us that the road to recovery is a spiritual path involving a relationship to your Higher Power, a loving relationship to your fellow humans, and a set of guidelines (12 Steps and Torah) for how to attain these relationships. The need to carry this message to others and to practice the principles implies the necessity of taking responsibility. The idea of responsibility is sometimes a frightening one. Many in recovery know too well how easy it is to become so responsible for a friend or spouse that we become enmeshed with them, or try to control them. What we learn from Step 12 is that while we must take responsibility for our own thoughts, feelings and actions by practicing the principles of our spiritual awakening, we must also go out and teach others. We are responsible to others for clearly defining our program of recovery and sharing it with them, but we are not and ultimately cannot be responsible for the choices others make about how they will live their lives.

Step 12 also points to the importance of the idea of community. Community is the place where we struggle with our spiritual awakening, with standards for our behavior (our moral and ethical path), and with the meaning of life. Practically this step implies that we have a responsibility to "care-front" (caringly confront[30]) those with addictions. We are responsible to those in our community. We cannot control them, but we cannot ignore them either. We must work to create a community of peace, compassion and recovery.

SOURCES:

1. All Israel is responsible (literally, "bound up with") one for the other.
   (Talmud, <u>Sanhedrin</u> 27b commenting on Leviticus 26:37)

2. Hillel Said: Do not separate yourself from the community; ... do not say, When I am free I will study, for perhaps you will not be free.
   (<u>Ethics of the Fathers</u>, ch 2:5) (see also 4:7)

   Spirituality cannot be attained in isolation from others. It is not purely personal.

3. Simon the Just was one of the survivors of the Great Assembly. He used to say: "The world exists because of three things: *Torah* (a moral and ethical path), *Avodah* (service to God), and *Gemilut Hasidim* (deeds of loving kindness)."
   (*Ethics of the Fathers*, ch 1:2)
   These three elements, God, Torah, and Israel constitute the three pillars of Jewish spirituality.

4. Hillel said: "If I am not for myself who will be for me, and if I am only for myself what am I, and if not now when?"
   (*Ethics of the Fathers*, ch 1:14)

5. You shall surely reprove your neighbor.
   (Leviticus 19:17)
   This verse from the *Torah* as well as source 1 (above) inform us that it is a *mitzvah* to be concerned about our friends and family. While we can never be responsible for someone else's inappropriate behavior, we do need to inform those who have gone astray of their error. Maimonides, in *Mishneh Torah*, Laws of Ethics, chapter 6 gives a number of guidelines relating this *mitzvah* to step 12. These guidelines are stated here as sources 6-9.

6. (6:6) When a man sins against another, the offended person should not hate the offender and keep quiet, as it is told about evildoers: "Absalom said not a word to Amnon, good or bad, for Absalom hated

Amnon." (II Samuel 13:22) But it is his duty to let him know and say to him: "Why did you do this to me? Why did you sin against me in this matter? For it is written: "You must reprove your fellow man." (Leviticus 19:17) If he has repented and asked for forgiveness, he should be forgiven. The person who so forgives must not be cruel, as it is written: "Abraham prayed to God" (for the man who wronged him) (Genesis 20:7).

7. (6:7) When a person sees that his comrade has missed the mark or has gone down the wrong path, it is a *mitzvah* to assist him in turning to the right path by pointing out to him that he wrongs himself (literally: "misses his own mark") by his bad behavior.

8. (6:8).... The sages declared: "Whoever shames anyone in public has no share in the world to come" (*Talmud*, Bava Metziah 59a). One should therefore be careful not to offend anyone in public, whether young or old. One must not call a person by a name of which he feels ashamed, nor state in his presence anything that would be embarrassing to him.
     We are reminded of the need to maintain confidentiality
     and the anonymity of all who attend 12 step meetings.

9. (6:9) If an offended person does not want to rebuke or say anything to the offender, because the sinner is ignorant or mentally disturbed, and warmly forgives him without resenting or rebuking him, then this is a demonstration of extraordinary loving kindness. The Torah objects specifically to bearing a grudge.

PROCESS: *Doing Step 12*

1. Take some time to review your practice of the 12 Steps and Jewish
   spirituality in your practical affairs. Make note of any opportunities you
   have had for carrying the message to others. Share your review in
   group.

   _____

   _____

   _____

   _____

   _____

   _____

   _____

   _____

   _____

   _____

   _____

   _____

   _____

   _____

2. Try the following imagery exercise. Relax, close your eyes. Take three
   slow breaths, taking longer to exhale than to inhale… Picture a
   calendar….. Let the pages flip forward into the future to the time when
   you have two solid years of recovery… See yourself going through your
   day…. See yourself encountering the people you normally see, the
   frustrations you normally encounter, and see yourself practicing all the
   principles of recovery which you have practiced in this program….
   See which principles and practices are most important for you…. Look
   back over the prior two years and back to the present time…. See what
   you have done to get here…. See the obstacles you encountered and
   what you did to get to recovery and peace/shalom…. When you are
   finished, write down what you have discovered. Share with your group.

   _____

   _____

   _____

   _____

   _____

   _____

Appendices

SPIRITUAL BOUNDARY MEDITATION

The Twelve Steps provide a framework for recovery which must be kept in mind at all times. Maintaining this awareness is a daunting task. The visualization presented here is intended to be used as a cognitive anchor. A cognitive anchor gives you a means to organize your experience and an easy means of accessing a complete meditative experience.

The meditation is based on a passage in the Talmud which is recited before retiring at night. (see page 63) I refer to this meditation as the Spiritual Boundary Cube Meditation because the cube provides a simple means to organize the concepts. Placing your self in the center of the cube and seeing yourself surrounded by angels and the spiritual tools of steps and *mitzvoth* creates a strong sense of spiritual boundaries. Spiritual boundaries tell us what is good and essential to incorporate into your recovery, and what is harmful, superfluous, and in need of exclusion. [31] Feel free to think of angels as heavenly 'beings' or as spiritual energy.

Instructions:

Imagine a cube surrounding you. On each side of the cube you will place specific thoughts and feelings related to your spiritual boundary. For each side of the cube described below, the first line gives the name of the corresponding angel with a translation of the name and its intention from the traditional meditation. The next line provides the 12 step related concept. The third line gives some of the related *mitzvoth* from the Torah.

Begin by learning the names of the angels and their meanings, using this alone as your meditation. As you continue your regular practice of this meditation over a period of several weeks, you can gradually add in the steps related to each face of the cube and then the *mitzvoth*.

This meditation/visualization can be used in a variety of ways. It can serve as a morning meditation to establish your connection to your Higher Power. It might be used as part of a stress management program. When you become tense you can begin a series of basic relaxation exercises and then add this meditation to help you visualize the source of your tension and ways to relieve it.

Spiritual Boundary Meditation

In the name of *HaShem*, the God of Israel,

At my right -
- *Michael* - Who is like God in love and support. (Feel yourself filled with Divine love.)
- Love of God as we understand Him/Her; improving contact with our Higher Power through prayer and meditation. (Step 11)
- "Love *HaShem* your God with all your heart, soul, might." (Deuteronomy 6:5)

At my left -
- *Gavriel* - God is my strength and discipline (Feel yourself filled with Divine strength.)
- Accountability to your Higher Power through moral inventory (steps 4 & 10), and admitting our wrongs. (5)
- "What does *HaShem* your God ask of you, but to fear/revere Him…" (Deuteronomy 10:12)

Before me -
- *Uriel* - God is my light. (Feel yourself filled with Divine wisdom.)
- Came to Believe (saw with God's light) in a Higher Power that can restore us to sanity. (Step 2)
- *Shema* "Hear Israel, *HaShem* is our Higher Power, *HaShem* alone" (Deuteronomy 6:4) - Reciting the *Shema* is traditionally referred to as *Kaballat Ol Shamayim* - taking on the yoke of Heaven, or in our context, deciding to stay in contact with our Higher Power.

Behind me -
- *Rephael* - God is my source of healing.
- Shielding our selves from our addictions through our spiritual awakening, 12 step work and practice (Step 12). Experiencing the healing power of *teshuvah* through readiness to have our Higher Power remove our defects (6), asking God to remove our shortcomings (7), and becoming willing to and making amends (8 & 9).
- "You shall not stray after your heart and after your eyes." (Numbers: 5:39)

Above my head –
- *Shechinat El* - God's Presence.
- We turn our will and our lives over to the care of God as we understand Him/Her. (Step 3)
- "I am *HaShem* your God who has taken you from Egypt (from addiction). (First commandment: Exodus 20:2)

Below me -
- (No representation as these concepts are excluded from our core spirituality)
- The belief that all our addictions (alcohol, drugs, power, perfection, etc.) are false gods which make our lives unmanageable. (step 1)
- "You shall have no other gods before Me." (Second of the 10 commandments: Exodus 20:3)

HEART

HEART is a mental imagery tool for coping with the impulse to turn to your addiction. Each letter of the word HEART represents the first letter of a step in the meditation. Rehearse HEART at least once an hour for one day, then twice a day for one week, and finally once daily for a month so that you will be able to use it whenever you feel an urge or impulse to act out your addiction. Prepare to use HEART by knowing the feelings which trigger your addictive behavior, preparing appropriate personal affirmations, and deciding what positive actions you can take to redirect yourself to your Higher Power.

H Visualize a **HEART** with an arrow pointing to your Higher Power. The HEART symbolizes your awareness that your life has become unmanageable and that you intend to turn your life and will over to your Higher Power.

E **Explore** the situation and feelings which are generating your current negative urge or impulse. Explain to yourself what feeling the addiction is covering up. Some of the core feelings that may trigger addictive behavior are

disregarded	devalued
unimportant	rejected
accused	powerless
guilty	unlovable
untrustworthy	ashamed

Explain to yourself that the feelings are simply your own emotional response to the situation. Let yourself know that having a variety of negative thoughts and feelings is a common experience. Thoughts and feelings constantly come and go in the mind, and you can have them without acting on them.

A **Affirm** that you are created in God's image. Nothing can change that. You have free will and are responsible for your thoughts, feelings, and actions. See the affirmations in Steps 6-7 for help.

Make several positive **affirmations** about yourself; e.g. In spite of what is happening, I can do ..., I can grow by..., I can take care of myself by .... or I can see this positively as ....   (Refer to steps 6 & 7 for help.)

R   **Rehearse** the positive action step you will take to Return to God / your Higher Power. This action can be saying an affirmation, reading a prayer, meditating, exercising, talking to someone, or any constructive activity. **Ready** yourself to have God remove this defect of character.

T   **Take Action**   Do the action you rehearsed and

Tefillah - Prayer.   Pray to your Higher Power asking for additional help if necessary or giving thanks for being able to do *Teshuvah*/turning.

Tzedakah - Do a favor for yourself or someone else. Put a few coins in the Pushkah (coin box for charity).

Two formulas to remember

Addiction = a vulnerable feeling + habitual behavior which numbs or avoids the feeling.

Recovery = Recognition of your own feelings + constructive action and thought = turning to your Higher Power.

CODEPENDENCY: A SPIRITUAL STRUGGLE[32]

In the 1980s and 1990's increasing numbers of individuals identified themselves as codependent. Codependents Anonymous (CODA) groups developed in all areas of the country.

What is codependency and why are so many people talking about it? Although the term originally referred to a person in a relationship with someone with an addiction problem, the term has expanded broadly to include any problems associated with focusing on the needs and behavior of others.

Codependency refers to a cluster of personality traits which are a result of inadequate psychosocial, spiritual and moral development. Codependents frequently suffer from low self esteem, take on the feelings and thoughts of others as their own, have difficulty making decisions, respond in extreme emotional fashion, have difficulty asking for what they need, and exhibit a variety of other maladaptive emotional patterns.

Issues of abuse and shame are central to the development of codependency and distinguish it from common neuroses. Codependency often has its origin within dysfunctional family systems, families in which children are ignored, abandoned emotionally, or abused in some physical, sexual, emotional, or intellectual manner. Normally, when a child or adult has behaved inappropriately the awareness of guilt feelings or shame helps the person to get back on the proper path. In dysfunctional families shame and guilt are often linked to behavior for which the person cannot be appropriately accountable. Either a person feels guilt and shame for behavior which is not their own or for behavior which really isn't wrong. For example, a child may be blamed for and shamed by a parent's drunken rage. At times children may be blamed and shamed for failing to live up to unrealistically high expectations.

The result of dysfunctional shame and guilt is that the person thinks and feels that he or she is worthless, deficient, and shameful. The dysfunctional guilt and shame of abuse cannot be challenged directly so the individual often resorts to passive or indirect methods of dealing with the shame and guilt. Some examples of passive or indirect solutions are social withdrawal, adapting to what others need and want at the expense of one's own needs and wants, and destructive self-expression such as addictions and compulsions. All of these solutions grow into codependent symptoms.

One of the most frequent dilemmas faced by the codependent individual is whether or not doing something for others is a virtue or codependency. Similarly, is doing something for oneself appropriate or selfish? The answer to these questions is itself a question asked by one of our rabbis two thousand years ago: "If I am not for myself, who will be for me? If I am only for my self, what am I?" Finding the balance is difficult work, as anyone with an addiction will testify.

Social factors may have played a role in the burgeoning of codependency. We have developed a corporate, highly mobile society in which economic and technological change goes hand in hand with changing family roles. These factors have led many Americans to experience tremendous feelings of isolation and loneliness which further feed the distortion of family relationships. These factors may influence the current high rates of addiction and codependency.

Individuals identified as codependent come to therapy with a wide variety of complaints including depression and various anxiety disorders. Treatment usually includes education, psychotherapy, and participation in CODA, a 12 Step support group which helps clients to overcome feelings of isolation and alienation. Therapy helps the individual deal with issues of personal shame, responsibility, and self worth, with the goal of improving self awareness, self assertion, self expression, and self caring. The recovery process is inherently spiritual and involves commitment to a Higher Power in place of an addiction to a substance or activity.

For the codependent who feels shameful, worthless, and lost in the shuffle, the tasks of building a positive identity and finding a spiritual path will be both difficult and rewarding.

RELAXATION RESPONSE

The Relaxation Response has been developed by Herbert Benson, MD, based on his research into meditation practices in a wide variety of cultures and religions. The Relaxation Response reflects the most effective common elements of these practices. It has been found to be beneficial in promoting general health and well being, fighting illness and reducing stress. Benson advises that the Relaxation Response is most effective when it is linked with the user's personal belief system, utilizing what he calls the faith factor. These are the procedures for the Relaxation Response:

1. Pick a focus word or phrase that is rooted in your personal belief system, short enough to be said silently as you exhale normally. Some suggestions Benson offers and others from Jewish tradition include:
    Echod (The Hebrew word for "one")
    Shalom (The Hebrew word for peace)
    The Lord is my Shepherd.   (Psalm 23)
    Serve the Lord in gladness.   (Psalm 100)
    Etz Hayim He Lamachzikim bah.   It (Torah) is a tree of life
           to those who cling to it.
    Ana El Na, Refa Na La (lo). Please God, Heal her (him).
    Give thanks to the Lord; for He/She is good.   (Psalm 136)
    Elohai neshamah sheh-natata be t'horah he.
        My God the soul which you placed within me is pure
        (From the Morning prayers, traditional Siddur/prayer book)
    Kol ha-neshamah t'hallel Yah.   With every breath I will praise *Yah*
    (God). (Psalm150)
2. Sit quietly in a comfortable position.
3. Close your eyes.
4. Relax your muscles.
5. Focus your awareness on your breathing. Take three slow breaths with each exhalation slightly longer than the inhalation. Then continue breathing at your normal, slow pace. Simultaneously, repeat your focus word or phrase as you exhale. Use one word or phrase during all of your sessions so that you will automatically come to associate it with the calming impact of the Relaxation Response.
6. Assume a passive attitude, and if other thoughts intrude in your mind, gently disregard them.
7. Continue for 10 to 20 minutes.

Practice the Relaxation Response once or twice daily. When the technique has been thoroughly learned it can be used to manage anxiety reactions. Benson's advice, when you feel anxiety being aroused, is to "say to yourself, 'Okay, stop!' Then, take a deep breath and hold it. Breath out very slowly and say silently to yourself the word, phrase, prayer, or sound that you normally use to elicit the Relaxation Response." Books by Herbert Benson, MD include *The Relaxation Response* and *Beyond the Relaxation Response*.

For those who wish to learn more advanced meditation techniques the Center for Spiritual Intelligence has a variety of books, classes and individual instruction programs that can be found at www.spiritualintelligence.com.

TOOLS FOR GROUPS

The information sheets which follow were used each week in SHOFAR. They are included here to help facilitate the development of new groups using the *Pathways to Recovery* model. The SHOFAR format is meant to be a guide which can be adapted to the needs of different groups. Select those segments which match the needs of your group members and the time limits for your group. Sharing takes place at every meeting. Before Jewish holidays, members of Shofar often requested that the group take some time in addition to or in place of the Step Study to discuss the meaning of the holiday and its significance for recovery. This instructional segment of the group can be readily adapted to meet members' needs.

SHOFAR   Meeting Format

Welcome to this evening's open meeting of the SHOFAR group. SHOFAR stands for Support and Help Organization for Addiction and Recovery.
My name is _____. I am your leader for this meeting.
We open our meeting with a moment of silence, followed by the Serenity Prayer.

> God, grant me the serenity to accept the things I cannot change,
> The courage to change the things I can,
> And the wisdom to know the difference.

SHOFAR is a fellowship of Jews in 12-Step Programs who meet to share their recovery, strength and hope with each other in a Jewish context. So long as we focus on recovery, we share a commonality that would otherwise not be present.

SHOFAR is not intended to be a substitute for regular 12-Step Meetings, but an adjunct to them. We believe that each of us needs the ongoing strength that comes from the respective fellowships.

Although SHOFAR is not a 12-Step Fellowship, we have borrowed two of their traditions as our guidelines. First is anonymity. We respectfully ask that you allow us the freedom to speak openly without fear that our privacy will be jeopardized. As in A.A., "Who you see here, what you hear here, when you leave here, let it stay here."

Secondly, we ask that the Seventh Tradition, to be self-supporting, be observed as well. We need your contributions to maintain our operations. Kindly remember this later in the meeting.

At this time we will go around the room and introduce ourselves so we can better get to know each other. If this is your first SHOFAR meeting, please let us know so we can welcome you.

Would _____ please read our "Statement of Purpose"? [On separate page]

We have a tradition of no cross-talking at our meetings. We do not comment, judge, criticize or give advice regarding someone else's feelings, thoughts or experiences. We focus our comments on our own recovery, thoughts, and feelings.

[SHOFAR   Meeting Format, page 2]

TORAH STUDY
We begin our meeting with learning from our tradition. Will _____ please read the selection on the weekly Torah Portion from *Living Each Day*. [Readings from other books may be substituted depending on the interests of the members.] Following the reading please share your thoughts and feelings about how the reading relates to your recovery. Feel free to ask questions about the content of the reading.
[20 minutes]

SHARING
We will now begin the next segment of our meeting, a time for sharing our thoughts and feelings about our individual recovery. We request that your sharing be focused as much as possible on your recovery process. Before we open up the sharing to anyone in the group, does anyone have a "burning desire" or a matter of personal urgency to share with the group? [30 minutes]
   [After all "burning desires" have been voiced, proceed with:]
Does anyone else have anything to share or have a positive recovery experience from the past week?

BUSINESS
The Seventh Tradition states that we are self-supporting. Donations may be placed in our "Pushkah" which we will pass around as we take time for any announcements or discuss any decisions to be made. [5 minutes]

STEP STUDY
We now continue with our current studies and discussion of the Twelve Steps from a Jewish perspective. [30 minutes] [This section may be done instead of the Torah Study section]   [Do one or both of the following as time and resources allow:]
1. At this time we may ask our Rabbi/teacher questions relating to Judaism and recovery to better our understanding.   [If no questions then proceed to number 2.]
2. Would _____ please read today's passage from *Pathways to Recovery*.   At this time we briefly share our reactions and thoughts about this passage.
   We wish to thank everyone who has read, shared and helped in any way during this meeting.

CLOSING
May God bless you and keep you.
May God's Presence shine upon you and be gracious to you.
May God's Presence be with you and give you peace. Amen.
         OR [A prayer of your choice]

SHOFAR Statement of Purpose

SHOFAR is a fellowship of Jews in 12-Step Programs who meet to share their recovery, strength and hope with each other in a Jewish context. We seek to explore our recovery as Jews, as our dysfunction in life may have alienated us from our heritage, our people, and from God.

We are taught that Torah, the Bible, is "*Etz hayyim he le-ma-cha-zee-kim bah* - a tree of life for those who hold to it." Therefore, through this fellowship we seek to obtain knowledge of our religious heritage, an awareness of who we are as responsible Jewish adults, and to find our own place within the Jewish community. If knowledge is freedom, then all we seek is to learn, so we may freely choose our path in life.

Meeting Times

The **SHOFAR** Program will hold weekly support group meetings at [*insert your location*]. The group is open to Jews in any Twelve Step program. Meetings deal with common interests for Jews in recovery and their families. Jewish values and spirituality are stressed. Each meeting provides an opportunity for sharing personal concerns and for working one of the Twelve Steps.

Sharing Guidelines

Please consider the following guidelines to help keep your sharing focused on Recovery.
Select an incident you want to share about.
When you share include your reflections on any or all of these questions:
Which Step does your comment relate to?
What positive idea, principle or practice have you learned from the step?
What 12-step or Torah principle can you relate to your comment or use to improve yourself or your behavior ?
[Time limit: 3-4 minutes.]

We Care Sign-In Book

Phone calls are a tool for recovery. While we don't have cross talk during the sharing segment of our meetings, you can use our phone list to call someone to ask for support or to give support. Look in the WE CARE book and make a note to call someone who has indicated s/he is feeling down, sad or lonely. [Your group may want to add e-mails addresses to phone numbers or use only e-mail.]

For Further Study

Ben Avraham, Rabbeinu Yonah. *Shaarei Teshuvah: The Gates of Repentance.* Jerusalem: Feldheim, 1967.

Benson, MD, Herbert. *The Relaxation Response.* New York: Morrow, 1975.

Berkovits, Eliezer. *Not In Heaven: The Nature and Function of Halakha.* New York: Ktav, 1983.

Buxbaum, Yitzhak. *Jewish Spiritual Practices.* Northvale, NJ: Jason Aronson, 1990.

Freedman, Manis. *Doesn't Anyone Blush Anymore: Reclaiming Intimacy, Modesty and Sexuality.* San Francisco: Harper, 1990.

Ginzburgh, Yitzchak. "And I am Prayer," *Ascent,* No 14 (V,2), Ascent Institute, Zefat, Israel. Winter 1988-89. pp 5-15.

Glass, Carol. "The Twelve Steps and Jewish Tradition." *JACS Journal,* II, 1, 1985.

Green, Arthur. *Seek My Face, Speak My Name: A Contemporary Jewish Theology.* Northvale, NJ: Jason Aronson, 1992.

Kadushin, Max. *Worship and Ethics: A Study in Rabbinic Judaism.* New York: Bloch Publishing Company, 1963.

Kamenetz, Rodger, *The Jew in the Lotus.* San Francisco: Harper, 1994.

Kantor, Matis. *Ten Keys for Understanding Human Nature: A Guide for the Entangled.* New York: Zichron Press, 1994.

Kaplan, Mordecai. *The Future of the American Jew.* New York: Reconstructionist Press, 1967.

91

Kaplan, Mordecai. *The Religion of Ethical Nationhood*. London: Macmillan, 1970.

Kaploun, Uri, Editor. *Lessons in Tanya: The Tanya of R. Shneur Zalman of Liadi Elucidated by Rabbi Yosef Wineberg*. Brooklyn: Society, 1982.

Luzzatto, Moshe Chaim. *Mesillat Yesharim: The Path of the Just*. Jerusalem: Feldheim, 1987.

Maimonides, Moses. *Mishneh Torah.*

Mellody, Pia. *Facing Codependency.* San Francisco: Harper and Row, 1959.

Mintz, Alan. "New Metaphors: Jewish Prayer and Our Situation." in Sleeper, James, and Mintz, Alan. Eds. *The New Jews*. New York: Random House, 1971.

Peck, M. Scott. *The Road Less Traveled*. New York: Simon and Schuster, 1978.

Peli, Pinchas. *Soloveitchik On Repentance: The Thought and Oral Discourses of Rabbi Joseph B. Soloveitchik*. Ramsey, New Jersey: Paulist Press, 1984.

Pirke Avot (Ethics of the Fathers) This is one of the Tractates of the Babylonian Talmud. It is included in many traditional prayer books for study on Shabbat afternoon.

Schlect, Dean. *The Way of Healing*. Unpublished manuscript, 1988.

Sherman, Nosson, ed. *The Art Scroll Siddur*, The Rabbinical Council of America Edition. Brooklyn, New York: Mesorah Publications, 1984.

Shneur Zalman of Liadi. *Likutei Amarim Im Igeret HaTshuvah v'Igeret HaKodesh*. London: Kehot Publication Society, 1973.

Steinsaltz, Adin. *The Thirteen Petalled Rose*. Northvale, New Jersey: Jason Aronson Inc., 1992, 1980.

Strassfeld, Michael. *The Jewish Holidays*. New York: Harper and Row, 1985.

The Torah, Philadelphia: Jewish Publication Society, 1962.

Twerski, Abraham, M.D. *Living Each Day*. New York: Mesorah Publications, 1988.

Twersky, Mordecai. *Heart Work*. New York: Global Village Music, 1987.

Notes

[1] *Pirke Avot* (Ethics of the Fathers), 1:2. *Mitzvah* is usually translated as "commandment". However, *mitzvah* can be seen as a deed connecting us to our Higher Power. Thus, every *mitzvah* is a spiritual deed.

[2] Spiritual Intelligence is a term which I coined and have written extensively about on my website www.spiritualintelligence.com. Spiritual Intelligence ® is also a registered service mark of Dr. Yaacov Kravitz.

[3] *Pirke Avot* (Ethics of the Fathers) 4:2.

[4] Rabbeinu Yona ben Avraham of Gerona, *Haarei Teshuvah: The Gates of Repentance*, trans. S. Silverstein, (New York: Feldheim, 1967), Second Gate: ch. 2, pp. 72 ff.

[5] Cited in Abraham Twersky M.D., *Living Each Day*. (New York: Mesorah Publications) 1988.

[6] Psalm 27, following the translation of Rabbi Mordecai Twersky.

[7] See Harold Schulweis, *Evil and the Morality of God* (Cincinnati: Hebrew Union College press, 1984).

[8] Op. cit. Twersky, p. 309.

[9] cf. Yitzhak Buxbaum, *Jewish Spiritual Practices* (Northvale, NJ: Jason Aronson, 1990).

[10] Adapted from Dean Schlect, *The Way of Healing*. Unpublished manuscript, 1988.

[11] See for example Rabbi Nosson Sherman, Ed., *The Art Scroll Siddur,* The Rabbinical Council of America Edition. (Brooklyn, NY: Mesorah Publications, 1984), pp. 107-108. The translation provided here is a modern adaptation and abridgment of the original Hebrew.

[12] See M. Luzzato. *The Path of the Just, Mesillat Yesharim:* The Path of the Just (Jerusalem: Feldheim, 1987), ch 2, pp. 28 -33. Chapter 3 deals with denial and distortion which often hinder our work with steps 3 and 1.

[13] See M. Scott Peck, *The Road Less Traveled* (New York: Simon and Schuster, 1978).

[14] Op. cit., Luzzatto, pp. 28-31.

[15] Op. cit., Luzzatto, p. 11.

[16] Suggested by Rabbi Aryeh Kaplan in his *Jewish Meditation A Practical Guide,* (New York Schocken, 1985).

[17] Adin Steinsaltz, *The Thirteen Petalled Rose*. (Northvale, New Jersey: Jason Aronson Inc., 1992, 1980).

[18] See Adin Steinsaltz, *The Thirteen Petalled Rose,* pp. 60-61, Shneur Zalman's *Igeret HaKodesh*, chapter 15; Matis Kantor, *Ten Keys for Understanding Human Nature: A Guide for the Entangled.*

19 Pia Melody, *Facing Codependency*, (San Francisco: Harper and Row, 1959).

20 Pinchas H. Peli, *Soloveitchik On Repentance: The Thought and Oral Discourses of Rabbi Joseph B. Soloveitchik*, (New York: Paulist Press, 1984), p. 78.

21 Adapted from David Burns, *The New Mood Therapy,* (New York: Harper, 1999).

22 My translation follows the teaching of Rabbi Y. Soloveitchik in Op. Cit., Peli.

23 *Ibid.*

24 Op. Cit. Twersky.

25 For more on this topic see Rabbi E. Berkovits, *Not In Heaven: The Nature and Function of Halakha.* (New York: Ktav, 1983).

26 Alan Mintz, "New Metaphors: Jewish Prayer and Our Situation." in James Sleeper and Alan Mintz,. Eds. *The New Jews,* (New York: Random House, 1971).

27 See Max Kadushin. *Worship and Ethics: A Study in Rabbinic Judaism,* (New York: Bloch Publishing Company, 1963).

28 *Ethics of the Fathers.* see also the Introduction to *op. cit., Luzzato*, pp. 10-13.

29 Numbers 15:39-41. Words in parentheses are my own interpolations.

30 Thanks to Jimmy Dan Sanders of the Pastoral Counseling and Education Center, Dallas for coining this term.

31 The idea of a cube and the specific *mitzvoth* assigned to each side is based on an article titled "And I am Prayer," by Rabbi Yitzchak Ginzburgh. *Ascent,* No 14 (V,2), Ascent Institute, Zefat, Israel. Winter 1988-89, pp 5-15. In order to integrate the material from the 12 steps I have changed the order of the *mitzvoth* as they appeared in Rabbi Ginzburgh's article.

32 This section is adapted from Yaacov Kravitz, "Codependency" originally published in *Shalom Rav* magazine, May, 1990.